Mastering Networking Basics From Novice To Pro

Book Wave Publications

Published by Book Wave Publications, 2023.

MASTERING NETWORKING BASICS FROM NOVICE TO PRO

First edition. September 24, 2023.

ISBN: 979-8223866367

Written by Book Wave Publications.

Also by Book Wave Publications

How To Make Money In Stocks Value Investing Strategies
Master The Steps To Move Away From The Past And Following Inspiration
Heartful Journeys: Exploring The Power Of Mindful Living
Essential Computer Networking Concepts You Should Know
Harnessing Your Inner Strength Overcoming Limiting Beliefs
Mastering Networking Basics From Novice To Pro

Table of Contents

What You'll Learn 1

About 2

Introduction 3

Fundamentals of Networking 4

LAN 6

WAN 8

Network Architecture 11

Client-Server vs. Peer-to-Peer 13

Architecture for Client-Server Networks 14

Network Equipment 16

Networking Speeds 17

OSI Open System 19

Network Layer 22

Transportation Layer 23

TCP 24

A Layer Of Applications 28

The Network Manager 29

Broadcast and Collision Domains 30

Tools For Networking 31

Network Cabling 37

Cable Fiber Optic 41

Advancements in Wireless 45

Wireless Equipment 46

SSID 47

Bluetooth 48

WiMAX 51

Radio Frequency Identification 53

Internet Protocol 55

Extending Wi-Fi Networks 56

IP Addressing 60

Configuring an IP Address 66

Using DHCP 68

Classes for Default IP Addresses 70

IP Subnetting 73

VLAN 79

IPv6 vs IPv4 82

Deal with Depletion 83

Protocols for Networks 84

Protocol for Frame Relay 91

Address Translation for Networks 92

Transport Protocols...96

Routing Desks 99

The Internet's Essentials... 101

DNS 107

World Wide Web: A Global Window 109

Communication 112

Visual Conference 114

Surveillance 116

Virtualization And Cloud Computing Architecture............ 119

Knowledge Of Cloud Computing... 120

Use of Cloud Computing 121

Virtualization.. 122

Vulnerability In Cloud Computing 124

Utilising Public Cloud Services 126

Private Cloud Services 127

Network Troubleshooting 128

Changing the Firmware.. 130

Hardware Upgrades... 131

Mechanics of Hardware.. 132

Troubleshooting A Network 133

Hardware Diagnostics 135

Network Management Synopsis 136

Troubleshooting Cable 138

Wireshark Quick Reference 139

Conclusion 140

Mastering Networking Basics From Novice To Pro

Learn The Fundamentals Of Computer Networking For Non-Techies

What You'll Learn

1. Understand How Computer Networks Work
2. Know the Inner Workings of a Computer Network
3. Understand the Benefits of Computer Networks
4. Know How to Effectively Plan and Design a Computer Network
5. Understand basic networking concepts, including switches, routers, and TCP/IP
6. Learn about network protocols including NAT, Ethernet, VLANs, VPNs, and DNS
7. Follow packets as they move through a network
8. Understand multi-destination traffic including broadcasts, unknown unicast, and multicast

About

Are you a non-techie who wants to understand computer networks? Are you a company person or prospective IT professional who needs to comprehend networks more fully? You've come to the correct site, then!

I'll walk you through the basics of computer networking in this Book, teaching you the fundamental core concepts you must understand. This Book is essential if you want to improve in or start a career in information technology (IT).

After completing this Book, you'll know how computer networks operate as well as how to plan and create one. What Are You Ready For, Then? Get In Today!

Who Should Take This Book:

1. Non-technical People Curious About Computer Networks
2. Business and IT managers who need to be familiar with computer networking
3. Inexperienced & Aspiring IT Professionals
4. Seasoned and experienced IT and networking professionals SHOULD NOT take this Book.

Introduction

You may be confident that reading this book will take you on a fun educational journey about a range of networking encounters. Networking for Beginners covers LANs and WANs, the OSI model, and networking components in exactly the right amount of depth while also clearly setting the pace with an uncomplicated explanation of networking's fundamentals.

It's also important to remember that network troubleshooting and maintenance have been trending topics. The Internet, wireless technologies, and the fascinating idea of virtualization in cloud computing have all received a lot of attention. The interesting ideas of IP addressing and subnetting are also introduced in this book, and they undoubtedly provide a practical touch to networking's mostly theoretical nature.

Networking for Beginners is a very practical and current introduction to computer networking for beginners in order to fulfil learners' current networking and technology expectations. The book was written from a teaching and counselling perspective, so the reader doesn't need to have any prior experience or expertise in the area of networking. The fundamentals of TCP/IP setup, router configuration, network troubleshooting, network security, IP Management, and other major networking subjects are covered, as well as the concepts of computer networking. You will have a firm grasp of a variety of networking protocols after reading this book, as well as how they contribute to the reality of the networking notion.

Fundamentals of Networking

The basic goals of computer networking, a broad field that encompasses many computing ideas, are communication and access to restricted (but shared) computer resources.

We'll look at the underlying ideas of computer networking in this chapter. The idea of a network is first discussed, then network architecture is examined, network administrator responsibilities are discussed, numerous LANs and WANs are listed, and peer-to-peer networking and client-server networking are contrasted.

We'll rapidly go over the different network building blocks, lingo, and the OSI model before concluding with a succinct discussion of collision and broadcast. Usually, the goal of this chapter is to give an overview of networking concepts and lay the groundwork for the subsequent chapters' more in-depth discussions of networking.

Computer Networking: Definition

Any group of computers that are connected to one another for communication, the exchange of data (and information), and other computing resources is referred to as a computer network. Due to the availability of additional network resources like file servers, printers, and many other hardware-based devices that may be shared, network hosts may be able to do more than merely exchange data and programs.

Computer networks may be divided into groups based on their size, purpose, and even geography. However, the primary factor used to categorise computer networks is their size.

The classification of networks demonstrates several prevalent network types: The WAN and LAN

WAN versus LAN

LAN stands for local area network, whereas WAN stands for wide area network.

LAN

Any connected computer network that is situated in a small space, such a home or business, is referred to as a LAN. Coaxial cables, twisted pair copper cables, and fibre-optic cables are regularly used kinds of communication medium that connect two or more computers in a LAN.

A LAN may be set up quickly and cheaply since it can function just as effectively with basic network components like switches, Ethernet cables, and network adapters. LANs can deliver data more rapidly thanks to the managed traffic.

LANs are generally simple to administer due to their simple configuration. As a result, by keeping a closer eye on what's happening locally within the network, security enforcement is improved.

Home networks and workplace networks are two LAN instances.

Benefits of LAN

Given that WANs have a limitless geographic reach in contrast to LANs' restricted worldwide coverage, LANs are undoubtedly superior than WANs.

A few LAN benefits are as follows:

Installation is simple since connecting computers only requires a little amount of space. Setting up a LAN is substantially simpler due to the lower number of networked machines in the constrained operational zone.

Because there are few networked computers and a limited network region, maintenance is simple.

The low number of networked devices and the relatively simple operating environment make security enforcement easier.

The Disadvantages of LAN

By considering both its geographical restrictions and the number of linked devices, a LAN's constraints may be summed up in a single phrase. This suggests that LANs are limited by their inability to support a large number of users, which limits their application to smaller workplaces, corporate settings, learning environments, and residential settings.

WAN

A wide-area network (WAN) is a type of computer network that links together several cities, states, and even entire nations. It outperforms LAN or MAN. There are no geographical restrictions on it. Through phone lines, satellite connections, or fibre optic cables, it connects vast geographic areas. One of the many WANs that are now in use throughout the world is the Internet.

In the corporate, governmental, and academic sectors, WANs are often used.

WAN examples

The examples below demonstrate how WANs may permanently connect individuals, no matter where they are:

Mobile broadband: 3G or 4G networks offer consumers in a sizable region, state, or even nation comprehensive coverage.

Private Network: Using telephone leased lines that they purchase from a telecom provider, banks build private networks to link their multiple offices that have been erected in various areas.

Last Mile: By simply connecting homes, businesses, and commercial structures with fibre, telecommunications firms provide internet services to thousands of clients in different cities.

Notably, the most well-known WAN that links individuals from all over the world is the Internet.

Benefits of WANs

WANs connect to enormous human populations spread across a large geographic area. The benefits of a wide area network may be summed up by considering how the Internet has affected people's lives all around the world.

data that is centrally located. WANs aid in the centralization of information and data. As a result, people no longer need to purchase backup servers for their emails and files.

Updates must be made to files. Since software operates on live servers, programmers may immediately access updated files.

exchanging messages in a hurry. WANs employ state-of-the-art hardware and software to facilitate message exchanges more quickly than on most traditional networks. Skype and Facebook conversations are two excellent instances of rapid message exchange made possible by the Internet, one of the most widely used WANs in the world.

Sharing of resources and software is possible thanks to WANs. Over wide area networks, resources like RAM, hard drives, and others may be shared.

business without boundaries. Due to the Internet, people who are geographically separated by the Pacific may now do successful business without ever leaving their current place. We do, in fact, live in a global community.

substantial bandwidth. Leased line users consume greater bandwidth. As a result, the company's output grows as data transfer speeds rise.

The Drawbacks of WANs

As the network grows, security problems become more serious. LAN and MAN security concerns are less critical than WAN security issues.

expensive installation fees. Setting up a WAN requires the acquisition of a significant amount of pricey gear and network management and administration software. Expensive mainframe computers, routers, and switches are required for the network to run.

Due to the network's extensive global reach, network issues are frequently a serious concern.

Network Architecture

All the resources required for the networking idea to operate to its maximum potential are included in the network infrastructure. In other words, what is typically referred to as network infrastructure is made up of hardware, software, network protocols, user input, and design features that enable efficient network operation, administration, and communication. The following are a few examples of network infrastructure components in a nutshell:

1. Hardware and software for networks
2. Internet protocols
3. Internet services

The hardware component of a computer network provides an interface via which users may connect network devices physically and use the network's services. The physical elements that make up a computer network are often considered hardware. Computers act as the host equipment for networks, which also contain routers, hubs, and switches as well as various peripherals like printers, wireless modems, network cameras, and file servers.

A Network Operating System (NOS) takes the first spot on the list of networking software. A NOS may not be required, however, depending on the structure of the network, especially in peer-to-peer network arrangements (covered in more detail in a subsequent article). In addition to a NOS, several software programs are installed on host machines for usage by the network to carry out various functions on the network.

Network protocols are rules and specifications that describe the specifics of how a network communicates. A protocol is a collection of conventions, practices, guidelines, and rules that directs network communication. In light of this, it should go without saying that knowledge of the two network models (TCP/IP and OSI) as well as network architecture, which explains the logical organisation of computers, is essential to comprehending computer networking as a whole.

A computer offers a wide range of services to its users. The role of the network (network function) is made up of all of the network services together. Data storage, directory services, email services, file-sharing services, and many others are examples of network services.

The OSI model, network speeds, the function of a network administrator, collision and broadcast domains, and peer-to-peer vs. client-server network topologies will all be covered in this part.

Client-Server vs. Peer-to-Peer

Architecture for peer-to-peer networks, All of the computers are interconnected in this type of design. All computers enjoy the same rights and are equally tasked with processing data.

Small computer networks with up to 10 PCs can benefit greatly from this type of network design.

There is no server role supported by the design. Each machine is given a set of unique permissions via an assignment. Unfortunately, when the computer containing the resource malfunctions or breaks down, problems do occur.

Peer-to-Peer Networks' Advantages

The key benefits of a peer-to-peer network architecture are as follows:

- Cheaper because there isn't a dedicated server.

- A minor network exists. As a result, managing and setting up the network is often simple.

- The operation of other machines is unaffected by the failure of one. As a result, it is quite trustworthy.

Peer-to-Peer Network Architecture Benefits

Centralised systems are absent from peer-to-peer setups. Thus, since every data is unique and stored in several places, there is no system for data backup.

No controlled security exists; each machine is responsible for its own security.

Architecture for Client-Server Networks

User computers (sometimes referred to as client computers) under this network paradigm depend on a main computer (the server) for resource distribution and security enforcement.

Security, resource, and overall network administration are handled by the server. On the other hand, client computers connect to the central computer or server to interact with one another.

For instance, if client "A" wants to communicate data to client "B," client "A" must ask the server for authorization. The server then responds by either allowing client A permission to communicate to client "B" or refusing them access. Communication can begin between client A and client y immediately or it may be necessary to wait for a while once the server gives client "A" permission to interact with client "B."

Advantages Of Client-Server Architecture

When a centralised system is present, data backup is possible.

Through effective administration and structure of network resources, a dedicated server enhances overall performance.

Since the central computer is in charge of managing all shared resources, security enforcement is enhanced.

Because requests are handled in an organised manner, resource sharing moves more quickly.

The Drawbacks of Client-Server Networking

Dedicated servers cost a lot of money. They make the network very expensive as a result.

Only trained staff members are allowed to manage the network. Client/server networks require experienced employees for efficient management, in contrast to peer-to-peer networks, which do not require any highly skilled personnel.

Network Equipment

Physically speaking, a network might be as straightforward as two computers linked together to transfer data through an Ethernet connection. That does not imply, however, that the network will remain straightforward. Because of this, even if a network building block is not used in the early stage of implementation, it should be taken into account in the original design.

Even if you are planning to build a home network or small office network, you should anticipate additional needs beyond those that are already planned for purchase and installation. You can either make accommodations for the immediate need for space, nodes, and wiring, or you can create a plan for future upgrades and additions. When a new server is connected without additionally replacing switches, routers, or hubs, it saves time in the long run and may reduce irritation.

Finding the appropriate networking components may be done by starting with the list below:

- Printers

- host databases

- PCs and client workstations

- doc servers

- computers, laptops, and mobile devices

Interfacing devices, hard drives, network switching and routing elements, webcams, network and end-user applications, and removable media are examples of additional peripheral hardware.

Networking Speeds

Although they are not completely interchangeable in computer networking, speed and bandwidth are often used synonymously. What then are bandwidth and speed?

Bandwidth is that "speed," which ultimately gets used, whereas network speed is the circuitry bit rate. Thus, bandwidth is the real throughput and speed is the prospective throughput.

The following terms (really bandwidth) can be used to characterise speed in the context of the internet:

- the speed at which a new connection may be made.

- how long it takes to comfortably stream a video.

- how quickly stuff is downloaded from a website.

- how quickly or slowly a webpage loads.

The "speed" of a network is greatly influenced by bandwidth. It is not absurd to claim that bandwidth is a data rate rather than a network interface (connection) in the context of computer networking.

There is a wide range of Ethernet network bandwidth, from a few megabytes per second (Mbps) to hundreds of Mbps. Wi-Fi standards and other networking technologies define various speeds (bandwidths).

Differences between theoretical and real network speeds are caused by a variety of variables. Some of the elements are:

- Internet protocols

- Overheads in communication between various networking gear components

- running programs

In addition, a discussion of network speeds would be incomplete without bringing up the concept of latency. It describes the period of time during which data is sent from a network host to a server and back. Milliseconds are used to measure it. It is occasionally referred to as a "ping," which needs to be captured at 10ms. It is thought that high latency will speed up and buffer.

OSI Open System

The full name of this idea is an illustration of OSI Open System Interconnection. The physical media required to transfer data and information from one software program to another in a totally different machine are shown in this model.

There are seven layers in this reference model. Each layer performs a certain purpose.

The International Organization (ISO) created the OSI Reference model in 1984. This is accepted as the main architectural paradigm for inter-computer communication in the present day.

The OSI model divides complicated tasks into 7 more manageable components. Each layer has a certain goal to complete and is assigned a variety of tasks. The tools needed for each layer to finish its task independently are also contained in each layer.

Details on the OSI Model

Upper and lower layers are frequently used to split the OSI model into two levels. The following distinct strata are found in the higher levels: Presentation Session for Transportation Applications. The following different strata are found in the lower layers:

Network's Physical Connection

This approach's upper layer largely deals with application-specific problems. These problems are resolved by the program. The application layer is the one that is above or closest to the user. Similar to how application software interacts with users, so do software programs.

When a layer is addressed in relation to another layer, it is referred to as the upper layer. Directly above another layer is considered to be an upper layer.

This method's lowest layer deals with problems with data transit. Both software and hardware are used to implement physical layers and data transmission. The physical layer is at the bottom of this paradigm. It also comes the closest to actual media. The physical layers give the physical medium the information it needs.

Functions Of Each Of The Seven Layers

Starting at the bottom and working our way up, we will concentrate on the distinctive functions of each layer of the OSI Reference model.

Machine Layer Data transmission: This identifies the type of data transfer—full-duplex, half-duplex, or simplex—that is occurring between two network devices.

Line Configuration: It provides a thorough explanation of the physical connections between two or more network devices.

Signals: The type of signals used to carry information depends on the physical layer.

Topology: The physical layer provides a thorough explanation of how network devices are configured.

Link Layer Data

This layer is in charge of making sure that data frames are sent via the network without any errors. Additionally, it establishes the network's data format.

The data connection layer ensures that network device communication is reliable and effective. It is in charge of giving each networked device a special identification number.

The following two layers make up the data link layer:

It transmits packets to the destination network layer at the logical link control layer. The packet header also yields the specific network layer address of the recipient. Flow control is used here as well.

The connectivity between the physical layer and link control layer is provided by the media access control layer. In this way, data packets are transferred via a network.

Actual Goals of Data Link Layer Framing: The physical layer's unprocessed bit stream is transformed into frames, or data packets, by the data connection layer. The data frame now has a header and trailer. The source address and the receiver address are both contained in the header.

Physical addressing: The frame must have a header in order to comply with the physical addressing layer. The recipient's address is shown in this header. The receiver whose address is listed in the header receives the frame.

The main responsibility of the data connection layer is to govern data flow. In order to prevent data corruption while in transit, it maintains a consistent data rate.

Error control: A cyclic redundancy check (CRC) is added to the trailer before the data packet is transferred to the physical layer. The recipient may request a new delivery of the incorrect frame if there are any issues.

Access control: This layer determines which network component, at any one time, has absolute priority over the link.

Network Layer

On the seven-layer OSI Reference model, it is the third layer. It controls how IP addresses are assigned to devices on the network and maintains track of where each one is located. The layers choose the best route for data transfer from the sender to the destination based on the network circumstances. Service priority is one of the factors that is taken into account while choosing the optimal course of action.

The router is one of the layer 3 components in charge of packet forwarding and routing. The routers that are utilised to provide routing services are described in the network layer of a computer network.

IP and IPv6 are the two protocols that are used to route network traffic.

The Functions Of The Network Layer

This layer ensures that the source and destination addresses are placed in the frame's header. The identification of devices on a network is made easier by addressing.

The network layer creates a logical connection between network devices through internetworking.

Frames from the top levels are received by the network layer, which subsequently packetizes them into packets. The Internet protocol is used to facilitate it.

Transportation Layer

It is the model's fourth layer.

The layer ensures that tasks are completed in the proper sequence. Because of it, data duplication is prevented. The major duty of this layer is to make sure that all data gets transferred.

The physical layer further divides data from the above levels into segments, which are smaller units.

For the reliability of the data, the layer enables end-to-end communication between the source and the destination. Another name for it is end-to-end layer.

At this layer, two procedures are employed:

users' datagram protocol for the transmission control protocol

TCP

TCP is the abbreviation for Transmission Control Protocol. It is a commonly used protocol that makes online data exchange and communication between systems easier. The connection between the hosts is established and maintained via the protocol.

Data is divided into segments, which are smaller data units. The produced portions go in various routes through the internet. They reach there in an arbitrary manner. To recreate the original message, TCP rearranges the individual segments at the destination.

UDP, or User Datagram Protocol

It is a transport layer protocol as well. The source is not notified when the destination gets data, in contrast to TCP. As a result, the protocol is now incredibly unreliable.

Operations for Transport Layers

The transport layer ensures that data is directed to the proper processes while the network layer controls data transit across systems.

It gets a message from its top layer for segmentation and reassembly. The entire message is then divided into multiple easily palatable components. Each segment is given a sequence number by the layer in order to be recognized.

The transport layer uses the segments at the destination point and the sequence numbers to reconstruct the original message.

Computers may execute many applications simultaneously thanks to service-point addressing. Additionally, it enables the transmission of data from one process to another and from one machine to another, all the way to the receiver. A port address or service-point address is appended to the packet by the transport layer.

Additionally, this layer offers data control. Instead of using a single targeted channel, the data is maintained throughout.

Connection control: The transporters provide both connectionless and connection-based services.

Each segment is treated as a separate packet by a connectionless service. The packets use a variety of paths to get there. The connection-based service, on the other hand, establishes a connection to the destination computer's transport system before delivering any packets. Every packet in the connection-based service takes the same route.

Error control is done end-to-end rather than over a single connection, much like data control. The message will arrive at its destination without interruption thanks to the transport layer at the source.

Typical Layer

The communication between network devices is established, maintained, and synchronised by this layer.

Functions of Session Layers

Synchronisation: During data transfer, the session layer inserts checkpoints one after the other. In the event that there are any problems along the way, the information is retransmitted from that particular checkpoint. Synchronisation and recovery is the term used to describe the complete process.

Conversation management is handled by this layer. By promoting communication between two processes, the layer is successful.

Alternatively, the layer may be thought of as approving interprocess communication. Half-duplex and full-duplex are the two alternatives.

The First Presentation Layer

The language and formatting of data transferred between two network devices are the main problems with this layer. It functions as the "translator" in the network.

An element of the operating system is the presentation layer. It is the operating system component in charge of transporting data between different display formats.

The Syntax Layer is another name for this layer.

The Presentation Layer's Function

On the destination computers, the layer converts data from sender-based forms into universal formats into receiver-specific ones.

Encryption

To protect data privacy, the display layer encrypts it.

Data given by the sender is altered into a distinct, independent form through the process of encryption before being transmitted across a network.

Translation

Information is sent between processes in various systems using character strings, character numbers, and a variety of other formats. Different computer systems utilise a variety of encoding techniques. As contrast to encoding methods, the presentation layer controls compatibility between them.

Compression

Before transmission, the presentation compresses the data. Bit loss is one of the components of compression. This step is crucial, especially when sending multimedia material like music and video files.

A Layer Of Applications

Users and apps can access network resources through this layer's interface. It deals with a variety of network concerns, including resource allocation, transparency, and others. This is not a request. It only performs its application layer function. It offers end consumers network services.

The Application Layer's Function

File access, retrieval, and management: This layer enables users to access, retrieve, and manage files remotely.

Mail services: This layer provides email forwarding and storage capabilities.

This layer provides the distributed database bases using directory services. In order to provide significant information about various items, this is crucial.

The Network Manager

A person is always assigned the duty of working persistently to make networking an exciting experience in order for a network to fulfil its tasks as intended. The network administrator is the individual who usually works in the background. A network operator makes sure the network is functional and up to date.

As part of fulfilling their duty, network administrators carry out a variety of activities. The primary duties of a network administrator are summarised as follows:

Storage on the physical network and cloud administration.

basic security enforcement and testing procedures.

helping network architects with the construction of network models.

Server administration and operating systems.

upgrading and deploying software.

troubleshooting a network.

network upgrades and maintenance.

setting up network software on servers, switches, and routers.

A network administrator has to have extensive IT knowledge and expertise, especially in computer networking. They must be able to think critically and have excellent analytical abilities to efficiently manage complicated network difficulties.

Broadcast and Collision Domains

The area of a network that is susceptible to network collisions is known as a collision domain. When two or more network hosts transmit data packets concurrently on a single network segment, collisions occur. It is important to realise that when collisions happen, a network's efficiency suffers. Networks that rely on hubs for communication with host PCs and other devices frequently have collision problems. Because hub ports are in a single collision zone, hub-based networks are more likely to have collision problems. When using switched and router-based networks, this is not the case.

In a broadcast, a message is forwarded. As a result, the network portion where a broadcast is repeated is referred to as a broadcast.

Every network device that uses a broadcast to communicate at the data link layer belongs to a broadcast domain. Switch and hub ports are automatically assigned to the same domain. Contrarily, various domains are assigned to different router ports. Additionally, a broadcast from one broadcast domain to another cannot be forwarded by a router.

Tools For Networking

Although there are both software and physical network components, the physical parts of a computer network are the main emphasis of this section. Host machines (computers), routers, hubs, switches, repeaters, Network Interface Cards (NICs), network servers, modems, and several other peripheral equipment make up physical computer networks.

Hosts that are PCs and workstations

The term "host machines" (or "computers") refers to desktop, laptop, and portable electronic devices (such as smartphones and tablets) as well as the supporting hardware they may incorporate, such as portable hard drives, CD players, keyboards, and mouse. Any computer network's hardware is mostly made up of these.

A network is nothing more than a pipe dream without computers. The key components are computers. Users can do a variety of tasks via the network using computers as a platform. Computers act as a link between users and the dedicated network server in a centralised system.

Network Interface Card (Network Adapter)

One piece of hardware that connects one computer to another on the same network is the network adapter, or NIC as it is more often called.

Network transmission speeds between 10Mbps and 1000Mbps are supported by the NIC.

The IEEE has issued a special address to each network card. These are used to identify every computer on the network and are referred to as physical/MAC addresses.

Network cards come in two different categories:

Adaptor For Wireless Networks

An antenna is included with a wireless NIC to allow users to connect to wireless networks. Most laptops come with an integrated network interface card (NIC), however certain desktop computers might need to have an external NIC installed. Thankfully, computer motherboards typically come with NIC ports for wireless NICs.

Ethernet Network Adapter

Almost all computers have a wired NIC that is permanently mounted on the motherboard. When using wired NICs, data is sent across connections and cables.

Hub

A hub separates many devices from a network connection. Cables connect every computer on a network through a hub. Each computer connects to the network via the hub.

When the hub gets a request from a specific computer, it broadcasts it to every network device on the whole network.

The request is examined by each network device to see if it is suitable. The request is denied in that scenario.

There are some drawbacks to this approach, including more bandwidth use and severely constrained communication. A hub is essentially outdated with the current buzz surrounding routers and switches.

Switch

A switch links many computer network devices together. This crucial connection device employs more sophisticated technology than a hub.

The ultimate destination of transmitted data is determined by an update on a switch. Depending on the physical address of each incoming request, the switch delivers a message to the specified destination.

It does not send data to every network device, in contrast to the hub. Data transmission rates rise as a result of each computer speaking directly to the switch.

Local area networks are linked to the internet through a router. It examines the packets before sending them to a different computer network.

It works at Layer 3, generally known as the network layer, of the OSI architecture.

The information in the routing table controls packet forwarding. A router is intelligent enough to select or decide the best route for data transit from all viable options.

Advantages Of Routers

Information and data transfers are highly securely guarded. Even though the transmitted data or information travels the whole wire, only the designated device for which the message is intended may read it.

It is dependable because when the router malfunctions or breaks down, only the affected network is affected, leaving the other networks it serves unaffected.

A router improves the performance of the entire network. If two or more connected devices create the same amount of traffic, the router can divide the network further into two equal "subnets." This lessens the additional traffic.

Greater network coverage is provided by routers without performance concerns.

Problems With Routers

Despite the fact that router downsides are commonly ignored, we'll only cover two here:

It costs a lot of money to use routers. Routers cost a lot of money. They raise the total cost of a network.

A competent crew is required. A network that is connected to a bigger network using a router cannot be managed by a novice or unskilled individual.

Modem

A modem is sometimes known as a modulator or demodulator. Through a phone connection, it converts digital data into analog impulses.

A modem and an existing phone connection can be used to connect a computer to the Internet. The PCI slot rather than the motherboard itself is where it is mounted.

Based on different speeds and data transfer rates, modems are separated into the following categories:

a network cable

a standard PC modem or a dial-up modem

cellular modem

Firewall

Firewalls can be either hardware or software. A firewall may be thought of as a hardware or software component of a network that controls access to and departure from a private network. The internet is frequently connected to private networks. When it's vital to prevent network users from getting illegal access to such networks, especially intranets, firewalls are quite useful.

The firewall is meant to be used to filter messages as they are transmitted into and out of the internet. Access to the firewall is restricted to those who meet specified criteria.

It should be made clear that aside from traffic filtering and network connection authorisation, firewalls do not provide authentication services. Therefore, they ought to be combined to provide stronger network security.

There are several kinds of firewalls. They include:

Using packet filtering in firewalls: Only accept packets that pass the necessary standard when they enter or leave a network.

Circuit-level gateway: When establishing a TCP or UDP connection, security procedures are necessary. The packets flow unchecked once the connection is established.

proxies with firewalls: In place of the host system, the proxy server establishes a connection to the internet and transmits requests. The configuration of proxy servers can be altered to filter the traffic that passes through them.

A web application firewall imposes a set of regulations on HTTP interactions. The guidelines are meant to identify and stop potential dangers.

Network Cabling

One of the most important components of computer networking is cabling. In order to link and act as communication media, the cables offer physical connections between various networking components. In other words, cabling serves as a medium for packets to be transported from a source to a specified destination as well as a means of establishing links between network devices.

Cables are categorised based on their nature and use. For the majority of networking tasks, Ethernet connections are often used. We'll talk about the following networking wires in this section.

Network Cables

Three main cable types are used in Ethernet wiring. They consist of Coaxial.

Copper twisted pair. Cables made of fibre.

Cables, Coaxial

Coaxial cabling is frequently used to provide internet connection. The fact that it contains two conductors running parallel to one another is what is referred to as coaxial.

Conductors that pass through the middle of coaxial cables are present. A layer of insulation is present around the conductor. A conducting shield is also included just after the insulating substance. Coaxial cables are extremely resistant to interference from the outside environment because of the insulating substance and the conducting cover.

There are two types of coaxial cables: thinnet and thicknet. While Thicknet is known as Thick Ethernet (10Base5) cable, Thinnet is known as Thin Ethernet (10Base2) cable. They are essentially outmoded Ethernet cabling methods.

Thicknet features a 0.5" diameter and uses Radio Grade 8 coaxial wire, which complies with the original Xerox Ethernet specification. However, thinnet is a Radio Grade 58 that is thinner and resembles Radio Grade 6 TV cable.

A thicknet may be as long as 500 metres and sustain data speeds of up to 10 Mbps. In a single second, this cable standard can accommodate up to 100 devices. Similar to thicknet, thinnet allows for speeds of up to 10Mbps. It can only stretch as far as 185 metres, however 200 metres was the intended length. Additionally, a thinnet can only accommodate up to 30 devices.

The primary attributes of coaxial cables are as follows:

Two conducting materials that are parallel to one another make up a coaxial wire.

The inner conductor and the outer conductor are two of the two conductors. While the exterior conductor is composed of a copper mesh, the inner conductor is constructed of a single copper wire. A non-conductor lies between the two conductors.

The exterior copper mesh serves as a barrier against electromagnetic interference (EMI), while the central core transmits data.

The frequency of coaxial cables is higher than that of twisted pair wires.

Pair of Twisted Cabling

Four distinct copper wires are found in twisted pair cables. The wires are wound in a spiral pattern. The twisting attempts to minimise crosstalk and outside interference. This kind of wire is frequently used in LAN deployments.

Both network cabling and phone cabling employ twisted pair wires. Shielded Pair Cables and Unshielded Twisted Pair Cables are the two categories. The former are frequently referred to as UTP cables, whereas the latter are known as STP cables.

Cables UTP

The usage of UTP cables is widely accepted in the telecommunications industry. They can be divided into the following groups:

Category 1: This is frequently used in telephone lines for slow data transmission.

Category 2: This one supports up to 4Mbps of data transfer rates.

Category 3: This one supports up to 16 Mbps of data transfer rates.

Category 4: This one is suitable for long-distance data transmissions and supports data rates of up to 20 Mbps.

Category 5: In comparison to the other categories mentioned above, it is capable of supporting data rates of up to 200 Mbps and even allowing data transfer over greater distances.

Advantages of UTP Cables

They are reasonably priced.

They can be effectively employed in high-speed LAN installations.

Installing unshielded twisted pair wires is simple.

The drawbacks of UTP cables

Due to their susceptibility to attenuation, they can only be used at close ranges.

Cables With A Shield

An insulating mesh covers the conducting copper wire in a shielded twisted pair cable to improve data transfer. They exhibit the traits listed below:

They are weakening susceptible. Hence the requirement for shielding.

Higher data transmission speeds are guaranteed via shielding.

Twisted pair wires with shielding are simple to install.

They are reasonably priced.

Compared to unshielded twisted pair cables, it allows transmission of larger data capacity.

Shielded twisted pair cables have limitations.

They are more expensive than cables with unshielded twisted pairs.

They have a significant attenuation risk.

Cable Fiber Optic

This cable transmits data by use of electrical impulses. The optical fibres in the cable have a plastic covering that allows them to transmit data utilising light pulses. Since it shields fibre optic cable from abrasive temperature variations and electromagnetic interference from other electrical connections, the plastic covering is very beneficial. Coaxial and twisted pair cable communications are far slower than fibre optic transmissions.

Parts Of An Optical Fiber Cable

Three parts make up a fibre optic cable: the jacket, core, and cladding.

Core

For the purpose of light transmission, this can be a thin glass or plastic thread. Increasing the size of the core results in a greater quantity of light passing through the fibre.

Cladding

This refers to the glass layer that is concentric. In order to facilitate the transmission of light waves through the fibre, it essentially provides a lower refractive index at the interface of the core.

Jacket

A jacket is a plastic protective layer designed to preserve fibres, maintain their strength, and absorb stress. The benefits of fibre optic cables over twisted pair copper wires will be discussed.

More Bandwidth. Higher bandwidth is offered through fibre optic cables. As a result, they transport more information than copper twisted pair cables.

greater velocity. Light signals are sent by fibre optic lines. As a result, as compared to transmission through twisted pair copper cables, optic data rates are particularly high.

As opposed to using twisted pair copper wires, data may be sent across greater distances.

Attenuation is less likely to occur in fibre optic cables. As a result, they are more trustworthy than twisted pair wires.

Compared to twisted pair copper connections, fibre optic cables are both smaller and more robust. Because of this, they can resist more draw pressure than copper twisted pair cables.

Cables With A Straight Through

An additional variety of twisted pair copper cable, known as a straight-through connection, is used to link a network host (a computer) to a router, switch, and hub. Patch cables are another name for straight-through cables. When one or more host computers connect to a router via wireless transmission, a patch cable provides an additional alternative for a wireless connection. Patch cables have matched pins. Additionally, it only employs the T568A or T568B wiring standard at both ends.

Overlay Cables

An Ethernet cable called a crossover offers direct connectivity between several networking devices. The RJ45 cable is another name for this wire. At its termination points, it employs two separate wiring standards: T568A on one end and T568B on the other. The internal wiring of a crossover cable reverses the receive and transmit signals. It is used to link networking devices of a similar nature. A crossover connection, for instance, can be used to link one computer to another or one switch to another switch.

Comparison of Straight-Through vs. Crossover Cables

Crossover cables and straight-through cables are typically used to connect comparable and dissimilar networking equipment, respectively. Therefore, straight-through would be useful for joining the following gadgets:

Switch from the server to the computer hub

Change the computer's Hub or Server

To the router

For the following networking device connection situations, crossovers are required:

- A hub-to-hub

- A PC to PC

- Turn on the hub

- Alternate switching

- Between routers

- PC NIC to Ethernet port on a router

Cable Rollover

In reality, rollover cables are "rollover wired cables." On their terminal ends, they have pin orientations that are the opposite. In other words, pin 1 on connector A connects to pin 8 on connector B. The main purpose of rollover wired connections, also known as YOST cables, is to connect to a networking device's console port so that it may be reprogrammed. A rollover cable is primarily used to establish an interface with a specific networking device, in contrast to crossover and straight-through connections, which are designed for data transfer.

Advancements in Wireless

Because it appears to be a more economical kind of networking, particularly when it comes to file sharing, access to digital media, and Internet browsing, wireless networking has developed into a fully-fledged IT industry. Wireless networking has undoubtedly altered the globe and will undoubtedly continue to do so in the years to come given the phenomenal expansion of mobile technology and the manufacturing of mobile devices.

The wireless industry has developed. The continual advancement of wireless technology is the most visible development. In this section, we'll concentrate our attention on the task at hand and keep an open mind while we explore the subtleties of the most widely applied wireless technology. We'll focus on the fundamentals of the three wireless technologies—WiMAX, Bluetooth, and RFID—in particular.

Additionally, we should bear in mind that wireless is the technology that is most susceptible to hacker assaults and infiltration before we become too absorbed in the topic of wireless technologies like Bluetooth, RFID, and WiMAX. Focusing on the premise that wireless network security must be sufficient is key. In fact, we'll look at potential wireless network assaults since they constitute a serious danger to the security and integrity of this already generally recognized "sub-concept" of the larger networking idea.

Wireless Equipment

Knowing that a wireless network is not actually wireless is useful. The wireless idea is made possible by a variety of hardware components. The most crucial hardware parts of a wireless network are as follows:

WLAN: Wireless network adapters are equipped with both transmitters and receivers. Once the adapters have been attached, the appropriate devices may communicate with one another by sending and receiving signals.

The difference between a wireless router and a wired router is that the latter has a physical connection to other network elements while the former does not. The router not only forwards packets but also acts as a hub for users to connect to other networks and the internet. Wireless network adapters are required for all devices that the wireless router supports.

Devices that increase the wireless network's range are called wireless range extenders. These might also go by the names range boosters or expanders. They increase the signal's intensity by amplifying it.

Wireless network devices called access points serve as connecting points. They link wireless clients to other wireless access points, Ethernet, and the internet.

SSID

The abbreviation SSID stands for Service Set Identifier. If we are aware that a service set in wireless technology refers to a group of wireless network devices, then an SSID is the technical name for a specific wireless network.

SSIDs are case-sensitive 32-character names. Special characters are permitted when SSIDs are generated.

The capacity of a Wi-Fi base station (wireless router) to broadcast its SSID allows devices with Wi-Fi capabilities to display a lengthy list of available wireless networks. In open networks, devices can just join if authentication is not necessary. In contrast, a secured network will ask for a passkey, without which a connection cannot be established.

Bluetooth

Instead of using a cable, 2.4GHz ISM frequency is used for data transfer in the IEEE 802.15 standard, the foundation of Bluetooth, which was created in response to the issue of cumbersome cabling that limited the connection-based requirements of mobile phones, computers, stationary electronic equipment, and a variety of portable device "networking."

Three different output power classes are possible because of Bluetooth technology. The maximum distances over which data may be exchanged are determined by the Bluetooth output power classes. The following is a list of the three output power classifications:

Power Class 1: This class of Bluetooth technology has a maximum output power of 20 dBm. Data may be sent up to around 100 metres away.

Power Class 2: This Bluetooth technology class's maximum output power is 4 dBm. Data may be sent from the gadget up to around 10 metres away.

Power Class 3: This class of Bluetooth technology has a maximum output power of 0 dBm. Data transmission from the source can reach up to around 1m.

How Are Bluetooth Devices Operated?

A device can look for any nearby Bluetooth-enabled devices that are within its data transmission range when Bluetooth is turned on. An active Bluetooth device uses the inquiry technique to look for other nearby active Bluetooth devices.

The initial Bluetooth device receives a response to the query when a Bluetooth device is located by another Bluetooth device. After a successful query answer, the paging process begins for both devices.

A link is created between the two devices during the paging process, and they synchronise. Once the connection setup procedure between the two Bluetooth devices has been finished successfully, a piconet is created.

An ad hoc network is known as a piconet. There can be a maximum of eight Bluetooth-capable devices in this network. All of the components of the gadget are just required to support Bluetooth. The Bluetooth feature is supported by a wide range of devices, including headphones, mice, telephones, and computers.

How to Establish a Bluetooth Network With Any Other Bluetooth-Enabled Device and Mac OS X.

Click Apple to choose "Systems Preferences" after that.

Select "Bluetooth" and then "Settings" from the list of available hardware options.

To turn on Bluetooth, click the 'Bluetooth Power' button in the pop-up box.

Click "Discoverable" to determine if adjacent Bluetooth devices can see your Mac OS X device.

Decide The Device You Want To Connect

If Bluetooth isn't already turned on, choose "Devices," then "Set-up New Device," and then "Turn Bluetooth On."

Following the aforementioned, the "Bluetooth Setup Assistant" will begin to walk you through the process of selecting your preference.

Cell phones, other devices, and keyboards are available alternatives. We must use "Other Device" as an illustration.

The Bluetooth Device Setup will find any new Bluetooth devices that the Mac OS X connects to. The screen shows a warning when another Bluetooth device is discovered. Select "Continue" to continue the pairing procedure if you want to use that specific device.

You can be asked for a "passkey" as a need for Bluetooth security, which restricts who can connect to your device. Only the owner of the "passkey" has the ability to link your device to theirs.

The essential stages for establishing up communication between two Bluetooth-enabled devices are, broadly speaking, as follows:

Turn on Bluetooth by finding the button in the settings of the device.

To make sure the devices are discoverable, turn on the "Discoverable" mode in the Bluetooth settings.

Choose your favourite Bluetooth device from the list of compatible devices before connecting.

WiMAX

These words make up the acronym WiMAX:

1. W-Worldwide
2. I-Interoperability
3. M-Microwave
4. AX-Access

WiMAX provides truly worldwide interoperability for microwave access as a result.

Broadband wireless access (BWA) was the primary use for which a wireless broadband was created. It is designed to be used as a wireless replacement for conventional broadband access for stationary and mobile stations. In the frequency range of 2GHz to 66GHz, it was found.

Broadband wireless connections from fixed network stations may reach distances of up to 30 kilometres. Mobile stations, on the other hand, can connect wirelessly to broadband within a range of 3 to 10 miles.

The 3.5GHz frequency standard for WiMAX on the international market. The permitted and unlicensed WiMAX frequency bands, on the other hand, are 5.8GHz and 2.5GHz, respectively.

Research is being done to use WiMAX in the 700MHz frequency range in addition to the aforementioned.

OFDM is the signalling technology used by WiMAX. OFDM stands for Orthogonal Frequency Multiplexing Division. Because it offers improved non-line-of-sight, or NLOS, characteristics in the frequency range of 2.5GHz to 11GHz, this WiMAX format, IEEE 802.16a standard, was chosen.

In an orthogonal frequency multiplexing division system, numerous frequencies are actively used to communicate from source to destination. This is quite helpful when dealing with multipath interference reduction issues.

A system can utilise OFDM to select the best frequency for data transmission when there are problems with interference from other frequencies. WiMAX also offers a selection of channel widths that may be customised to WiMAX requirements globally to provide the fastest data transfer rates. channel sizes for 3.5GHz, 5GHz, and 10GHz. Additionally, IEEE 802.16a WiMAX's MAC layer is different from IEEE 802.11 Wi-Fi's. WiMAX just needs one entry to establish a network connection, in contrast to Wif-Fi. A base station gives WiMAX a time-space after it has connected to a network. As a result, WiMAX intended network access is granted by the base station.

There are working point-to-point and multipoint WiMAX networks. This is crucial in cases when DSL and cable network connectivity are unavailable. This wireless network technology, in large part, enables the last mile connectivity. A 40-mile travel limit is also present.

Radio Frequency Identification

This is a wireless network technology that is sometimes referred to as RFID and is generally used to identify and track people, animals, parcels, and other things via radio waves. The basis of this approach is the modulated backscatter idea. Simply said, "backscatter" refers to how radio waves are reflected when they come in contact with RFID tags. After reflecting, the radio waves then go back to the transmitter. The unique identifying data is included in the radio waves that were reflected after striking the RFID tag.

The RFID system is composed of the following two elements:

- A watcher

- An RFID tag

A reader is also known as a transceiver. This consists of an antenna and a transceiver.

The RFID tag is also known as an RF transponder. It consists of radio electronics and an integrated antenna.

Radio waves sent by the transceiver (reader) activate the RFID tag. The RFID tag then transmits modulated data and a special identifying code back to the transceiver. The transceiver extracts the modulated data from the RFID tag.

Features of an RFID System

The following are the three crucial components of an RFID system:

operation with regularity.

power sources for RFID tags.

a communication protocol, sometimes referred to as the air interface protocol.

Powering an RFID tag

RFID tags may be categorised into three groups based on how they get their electricity to work. The three types of RFID tags accessible are active, semi-passive, and passive.

RFID tags that are "active": These tags use batteries to power their ability to transmit signals back to the transceiver.

Semi-active RFID Tags: These tags' electronics are battery-powered, but they use the "backscatter" principle to send signals to the reader.

The rectification of RF energy from the reader provides the power for passive RFID tags. The RFID tag's circuitry may be operated and the radio signal can be sent back to the reader using the rectified energy.

Operation Period

RFID tags need to be tuned to the frequency of the transceiver in order to work. LF, HF, and UHF are the three frequencies that RFID tags may operate on.

Frequency shift-keying is used by low frequency systems to operate between 125 and 134 GHz.

High frequency uses the industrial band at 13.56GHz.

Ultra high frequency, or UHF, uses radio frequencies between 860 and 960 MHz and 2.5 GHz.

Internet Protocol

Slotted Aloha is the name of the air interface protocol adopted for RFID tags. It has a lot in common with the Ethernet protocol. According to the slotted Aloha protocol, RFID tags are only allowed to send radio signals when they are powered and at certain intervals after that. This technique considerably lowers the possibility of RFID transmission errors. Additionally, it enables the quick scanning of up to 1000 RFID tags in a single second.

Consumers may use WAPs to access the Internet even while they are on the go. For instance, someone may hang a special device from the window of their RV. It connects into a computer port and facilitates access to local area networks and the Internet when positioned close to an active WAP (as close as a few feet through obstructions like thick walls or as far as 400 or so feet in open space). If your wireless access device's signal is strong and reliable and you are close enough to a WAP to pick up the signal, you can easily connect.

Extending Wi-Fi Networks

When someone talks about wireless networking, they most usually describe using one or more Wi-Fi protocols.

They include the following protocols, which are most frequently used by home and small-office networks:

- 802.11g

- 802.11b

- version 802.11n

Even though they are somewhat complicated, these standards may be thought of as ones that make Ethernet networking possible without wires. The standards' radio wave level functioning differs; for the end user, the throughput speeds are the variable that stands out the most. The 802.11n protocol, for instance, increases data transfer by using multiple radio transmitters and receivers.

Even while they are unlikely to ever totally replace wired networks, wireless networks do provide a workable substitute for those in small businesses and home networks with a few nodes. The security, ease of use, consistency of data rates, and stability of wired networks will ensure their viability as a connecting option for the foreseeable future. In fact, some network topologies rely solely on wireless networks to provide connection, fully avoiding the use of wires. Wireless networks provide additional connection in a variety of applications. Additionally, public WAPs, also known as hot spots, which are frequently located at fast food restaurants, coffee shops, hotels, and airports, allow mobile employees and travellers to connect and stay in touch.

Note

When referring to wired networks, the statement "at wire speeds" is interpreted to imply that the network's cables and other hardware limit how quickly data may move across it. Fast Ethernet (100 Mbps) or Gigabit speed (1,000 Mbps) wired networking conncctions do not guarantee that the processor throughput will equal such speeds. Speed limiters in a wired environment might be anything from the cable itself to the network interface card's (NIC) capabilities to the CPU and system board of the computer's bus speed. Wireless networks, like wired networks, feature a carrier radio frequency that, in accordance with the different standards, is meant to convey data in the optimal conditions at the indicated data throughput. Your actual throughput will be reduced for all the same reasons as wired networks, in addition to the fact that the signals are affected by distance and by radio interference from other nearby wireless networks, portable phones, and even microwave ovens. A Wi-Fi device that should, for example, obtain 11 Mbps throughput most likely won't in a typical setting.

Ad Hoc Mode Versus Infrastructure Mode

In Ad Hoc Mode, a router or other device is used to operate wirelessly in a peer-to-peer setup without centralised administration. The connected gadgets of the ad hoc network exchange data directly.

Ad hoc networks may be set up quickly and just need a basic configuration. Therefore, they are ideal when a small, temporary LAN or an economical, all-wireless LAN implementation is needed.

To create an ad hoc network, the proper wireless adapters must be configured for use in the ad hoc mode. The devices on the ad hoc network must also use the same SSID and channel number.

Mode of Construction

When a wireless network is in infrastructure mode, a single access point serves as the hub for all device communication. The access point is frequently a wireless router. Devices send packets to the access point, which then receives and sends the packets to their designated destinations.

Wireless Network Security

Wireless networks are particularly susceptible to attacks. It is difficult to establish access limits on wireless signals since they may traverse the specified geographic bounds. This is especially true for persons who are motivated to break into the network.

Dangers To The Security

The typical threats to wireless networks include the following:

Aggression in a "Parking Lot"

Because wireless signals from access points go to places they are not meant to, wireless networks are excellent targets for hackers. Attackers would only linger outside a building (such in a parking lot) in parking lot attacks, taking use of the wifi signal that is available outside the structure's walls. They may swiftly breach the network's security, get access to its internal resources, and create havoc.

Shared Authentication Error

Passive assaults can be used by attackers to circumvent shared authentication. The challenge and response sent between an access point and an authenticating client might be overheard. The attacker could steal the data needed for authentication and use it to log into the network. This attack may be stopped by using data encryption between clients and the access point.

The Service Set Identifier has a bug

If the devices' default SSIDs are not changed, attackers may use them to enter the network. A defence against such attacks is to alter the device SSID on network devices.

The WEP Protocol's flaws

Wireless devices that enforce WEP for security enforcement on wireless networks are susceptible to eavesdropping since WEP is by default disabled on such devices. It is therefore required to adjust device settings such that they are unpredictable.

IP Addressing

What does IP stand for? An IP address is a four-octet, eight-bit digital address with a total of 32 bits, which appears as follows when typed out: 10.156.158.12. Evidently, an IP is a unique collection of dots-separated digits. When a computer (or other network device) uses Internet Protocol (IP) for network communication, the combination of numbers is used to identify it. Any octet, or group of digits, in an IP address can have a value between 0 and 255.

There are some similarities between an IP address and a phone number. You can call someone if you know their phone number, such as your Uncle Brown, by entering it into your phone's keypad. When you and Uncle Brown's phones are connected through an audio channel, the computers and switching hardware at your phone company go to work.

Once you're linked, you may talk to Mr. Bradley anywhere he may be in the world. When you do, the audio signal containing your voice will normally move from your home to a switch at your local phone company across two copper cables.

The signal may then be transformed into a light wave and sent from that point to another switch through a fibre optic line. In order to move from one microwave tower to another, the audio signal may be changed into a radio wave signal at this second switch. The signal will eventually be transformed back to an analog audio signal as it travels over two copper lines from Uncle Brown's phone company at her home, eventually reaching its destination—Uncle Mike's residence. (The usage of landlines is presumptive in this situation. The specifics of this method will change if cell phones are involved, but the overall idea will remain the same.)

What Purpose Does an IP Address Serve?

An IP address makes connections between computer hosts and routing hardware possible, much as how phones utilise numbers to communicate on a local, regional, national, or worldwide level. In other words, two computers connected to the Internet can interact if they know each other's IP address. However, as opposed to phones, which link via switching equipment, computers connect to one another through the Internet using routing equipment, which shares the communication pathways with tens of thousands or more other computers.

The task of a router is to locate a quick, open communication link to another router that is near to and connected to the target computer when data is sent from a computer to that router.

The router does this either via the use of default routes or by the dynamic learning and recording of tables, referred to as "routing tables," that track which IP addresses are present on any one of the many open, active, and running communication ports on the router. Data may travel via several alternative routes or paths to reach its destination if necessary since all of the routers connected together on the Internet resemble a spider's web. The other routers attempt to transport the data and look for an alternate path to the destination if one of the routers or another connected connection goes down.

Routers also assign IP addresses so that the dynamic communication technique can locate each other.

System of Binary Numbers

Let's define (or rather, describe) what a binary system is and what it means in terms of computing before getting into the specifics of how it operates.

What does "binary number system" actually mean?

The base-2 number system is used here. Gottfried Leibniz is credited with developing this type of numeric system. Every byte of binary code is built on the base-2 number system, which, as the name suggests, is made up just of the integers 0 and 1. It is the simplest number system. Binary code is the sole machine-readable code for all computer systems, as we all know (or ought to know).

Binaries in Use

Electrical ON and OFF signals are denoted, respectively, by 1 and 0. Normally, the 1 is moved one space to the left into the position of the 2 when one adds one to one. Then they substituted a 0 for a 1 in its place. The result is 10. Consequently, a 10 in the base-2 number system indicates 2 instead of 10, as it does in the decimal number system.

Place values start with 1s in the widely used decimal number system and gradually increase to 10s, 100s, and 1000s to the left. This is common since the decimal system is based on powers of ten.

Similar to this, the binary number system's place values start with 1s through 2s, 4s, 8s, and 16s, in that sequence, starting from the left. This is due to the binary system's usage of powers of 2. Bits are the binary numbers 0 and 1, respectively.

The Basics of the Binary Number System

Computers are fueled by electricity, and their circuitry is continually switching between ON and OFF. In order to represent numbers, letters, and other characters, computer equipment can work more effectively with ON/OFF electric circuit switching mechanisms.

System of Hexadecimal Numbers

We've discussed how the binary number system uses base 2, whereas the decimal number system uses base 10. In light of everything we've seen thus far, it is reasonable to assume that the hexadecimal number system is a base-16 number system, as the name indicates.

Ten numeric digits and six non-numeric symbols make up the hexadecimal number system. Consequently, it consists of 16 "symbols." After 9, there are only single-digit numerical values, hence the first six letters of the English alphabet—A, B, C, D, E, and F—are used.

Hexadecimal value in decimal form

An A 10 a B 11 a C 12 a D 13 an E 14 a F 15

Hexadecimal Operation

A nibble is a 4-bit number that represents a hexadecimal digit. The digit can be represented by the symbols 0–9 or A–F. When two nibbles are added together, an 8-digit value known as a byte is obtained. Bytes are commonly used in computer processes. Therefore, utilising a hexadecimal representation rather than a binary representation of numbers to express such big amounts becomes significantly more efficient. It's crucial to end or begin hexadecimal representations with "H" or "0x" to reduce the likelihood of misunderstanding. For example, h34, 0x605, 45h, or any other format in the range.

Standard Gateway

If there is no alternative path specification that matches the IP address of the receiving network host, the default gateway utilises the IP suite to function as a router and sends packets to a computer on a separate network.

Locating The Default Gateway's Ip Address

For efficient network troubleshooting and to access web-based router administration, it's crucial to be able to remember the default IP address of the network. The default gateway's IP address is typically the router's private IP address. It is the IP address that a router uses to connect to a different local network. The default gateway's IP address might not always match the private IP address, therefore you'll need to find it in some other means.

The procedure for locating the IP address of the default gateway (for all versions of Microsoft Windows) is as follows:

Start by launching the Control Panel.

In Windows XP, you must click on Network and Internet Connections. Next, choose Network and Internet.

The next step is to select Network and Sharing Center (Windows XP users should select Network Connections and proceed directly to step 5 instead of 4). In the Network Sharing Center, click Change Adapter Setting (or Manage Network Connection if you're on Windows Vista).

trace the IP connection to the default gateway.

Click the network connection twice. Depending on the network you're using, this may launch a window for Ethernet Status, Wi-Fi Status, or another dialog.

Choose Details (in Windows XP, Support tab, then Details).

Find the default gateway for IPv4 or IPv6, whichever you like.

The Value Column must include the IP address of the Default Gateway.

Note the IP address of the Default gateway.

The IP address of the default gateway may now be used to access the router, troubleshoot network connection difficulties, or carry out any other actions on the device.

How to Manually Find Your IP Address

Knowing your computer's IP address might be useful at times. Here's a quick method for determining the IP address that your computer has been given:

Click on Start->Run, input cmd, then hit the ENTER key to launch the CMD prompt.

Step 1's command prompt will appear. Type the command ipconfig/all there.

Your computer's IP address, DNS servers, default gateway, subnet mask, and many other significant network components should all be shown in a window. As an alternative, think about taking the following actions:

Ping the router's IP address, if you know it. Open the command prompt (just as in the previous way) to ping the router's IP address.

Exercise: You should be able to determine whether your system is correctly set up with an IP address based on what shows in the CMD prompt.

Configuring an IP Address

A step-by-step manual for setting the machines in our workplace LAN is provided below:

When using Windows 8 or 10, open the Control Panel, choose Network and Internet, click on Network and Sharing Center, click on Local Area Connection, select Properties, and then click Continue (the window displaying the local area connection properties appears).

When looking at the Local Area Connection Properties Window

Double-click TCP/IPv4 to bring up the properties menu. From there, choose Use the following IP address. Type in the IP address and subnet mask. Then click OK.

When using Windows 7, go to Start > Control Panel > Network and Internet > Network and Sharing Center > Local Area Connection > Select Properties > Continue (the Local Area Connection Properties window opens) > Double-click TCP/IPv4 (the Properties menu opens).

Choose Use the following IP address, type in the IP address, and then hit OK.

There are very few variations between the procedures in various Windows operating system versions.

In Mac OS, choose Built-in Ethernet by clicking Apple, System Preferences, Network, and Network Status.

A new screen with the option to configure IPv4 displays.

Choose Manually, manually enter the IP address and subnet mask, and then choose Apply.

The setup of the LAN at the workplace mentioned above uses the subnet mask 255.255.0.0 (continue reading to learn more about subnet masks).

Dynamic Host Configuration Protocol is known as DHCP. A network's IP addresses may be distributed fast, automatically, and centrally thanks to this protocol. When the default gateway, subnet mask, and DNS server are set up properly, DHCP is also advantageous.

Using DHCP

We can go forward now that we are aware of what the DHCP performs. However, we are unsure of how it completes its task. I promise you that we won't leave here until we completely comprehend how DHCP operates.

DHCP Server A DHCP server creates additional network data and assigns distinct IP addresses automatically. When deploying big networks, a single dedicated computer may be used, as opposed to small enterprises and residences, which depend on routers to carry out DHCP server functions.

In order to obtain their IP addresses, clients on routed networks ping the routers. Any attainable IP addresses are subsequently sent via routers to the network devices that asked for them.

The inquiring devices must be logged in to the network and operational. The server must be the request's destination. A DHCPDISCOVER request is one example of this. The DISCOVER packet contains the DHCPDISCOVER request. A DHCPOFFER message is sent back to the client by the server in response, giving it an IP address. The proposal is then accepted by the network device as a response. If the server determines it is appropriate to verify the IP address issued to the device, it sends an ACK confirming that the device has been given the desired IP address. The server sends a BACK if it determines that verifying the device's IP address assignment is not appropriate.

Advantages of DHCP

It is not possible to use DHCP to assign the same IP address to several network devices.

Administratively, network administration is made simpler by dynamic IP address allocation.

For the DHCP server to assign each computer or device on the network an IP address (and enable network connectivity), they must all be configured appropriately.

Since other linked devices must continually update their synchronisation settings, stationary equipment like printers don't require their IP addresses to change frequently.

Classes for Default IP Addresses

The IP hierarchy lists several distinct IP address categories. Five distinct IP address types are recognized under the IPv4 addressing scheme.

Below is a list of the classes:

Class A, Class B, Class C, Class D, and Class E addresses are all types of addresses.

Category A Address

The following characteristics help to distinguish this collection of IP addresses:

A Class A network address's first octet's first bit is always set to zero. Therefore, the first octet of a network address falls between 1 and 127.

Class A addresses are only considered to be IP addresses with a starting address of 1.x.x.x and a maximum address of 126.x.x.x.

The 127.x.x.x IP range manages the loop-back IP addresses.

For Class A addresses, the default subnet mask is 255.0.0.0. The class A address network can thus only accommodate 126 networks.

When defining Class A IP addressing, the sequence 0NNNNNNN.HHHHHHHH.HHHHHHHH.HHHHHHHH is used.

Category B Address

The following characteristics help to distinguish this collection of IP addresses:

The first two bits of the first octet are constantly set to one and zero in a class B address.

The range of Class B IP addresses is 128.x.x.x to 191.255.x.x.

The subnet mask for Class B is set to 255.255.x.x by default.

214 (16384) is the standard for class B network addresses.

Each network contains 65534 host addresses.

Class B IP addresses are formatted as 10NNNNNN.NNNNNNNN.HHHHHHHH.

Category C Address

The characteristics of Class C addresses are as follows:

A network address's first octet's first three bits are always set to 110.

192.0.0.0 to 223.255.255.255 is the range of class B IP addresses, while 255.255.255.x is the class C subnet mask by default.

There are 221 (2097152) network addresses in Class C.

Each network contains 28-2 (254) host addresses.

Addresses in the class C are written using the format 110.NNNN.NNNNNNNN.NNNNNNNN.HHHHHHHH

Category D Address

The characteristics of Class D addresses are as follows:

The first four bits of the first octet of the IP address total 1110.

Class D IP addresses fall between 224.0.0.0 to 239.255.255.255.

Multicasting is only possible with this class. Data is transmitted to several hosts using multicasting as opposed to only one or two. It is not essential to differentiate between host addresses and class D IP addresses as a consequence. Additionally, Class D has no subnet mask.

Postal Code For Category E

The qualities of Class E include the following:

Class E IP addresses are reserved for testing, investigation, and research purposes.

These IP addresses are located in the range of 240.0.0.0 to 255.255.255.254. Class does not have a subnet mask, much like Class D.

IP Subnetting

What is Subnet? Your pool of IP addresses must be subnetted if you're using a routed IP system. This enables every subnet to perceive itself as a unique section of the overall internetwork. The router then unifies all of the subnets into a single network. Because it creates a routing table, the router is able to route traffic to the appropriate segment. The routing table essentially serves as the network's map.

Due to the complexity of IP subnetting, we will keep our talk to one class of IP addresses in order to keep it simple and understandable for beginners. As an example, we will use subnetting a Class B range of IP addresses. Although subnetting Class C networks severely reduces the amount of usable IP addresses you end up with, the same techniques we use to subnet the Class B network may equally be used to subnet a Class A or Class C network.

Subnetting involves two steps. The network's subnet mask must first be identified; it will differ from the usual subnet masks; for instance, the default subnet mask for Class B is 255.255.0.0. You must first determine the network's new subnet mask before calculating the range of IP addresses that will be present in each subnet.

Before we perform the calculations for subnetting a Class B network, let's have a little discussion. It will, in my opinion, help with the general comprehension of the subnetting procedure. Using a certain amount of bits for subnetting, the following basic explanation shows the new subnet masks, the number of subnets, and the number of hosts per subnet that would be produced:

When we utilise 2 bits, there are 3 subnets, 16382 hosts per subnet, and the subnet mask is 255.255.192.0.

When we utilise 3 bits, there are 6 subnets, 8190 hosts per subnet, and the subnet mask is 255.255.224.0.

When we utilise 4 bits, there are 14 subnets, 4094 hosts per subnet, and the subnet mask is 255.255.240.0.

When we utilise 5 bits, there are 30 subnets, 2046 hosts per subnet, and the subnet mask is 255.255.248.0.

When using 6 bits, there are 62 subnets, 1022 hosts per subnet, and the subnet mask is 255.255.252.0.

When 7 bits are used, the subnet mask is 255.255.254.0, there are 126 subnets, and there are 510 hosts per subnet.

When 8 bits are used, the subnet mask is 255.255.255.0, there are 254 subnets, and there are 254 hosts per subnet.

130.1.0.0 is our selected network as it is a Class B network. The third and fourth octets are represented by the first and second zeros, respectively. The host addresses are only allowed to use the third and fourth octets. To make class B subnets, we must take bits from the third octet. Remember that when more bits are borrowed, we build more subnetworks but fewer host addresses (this is clear from the discussion of Class B subnetting above). The IP address's network ID portion is also constant.

Borrowing a Bit

If our 130.1.0.0 network required the creation of 30 subnets, we would first need to calculate the number of bits that could be borrowed to create the subnet mask.

Since we are unable to utilise subnet 0, we must first add all lower order bits together before taking one out to determine the total amount of bits.

The bits are arranged as follows: 128, 64, 32, 16, 8, 4, 2, and 1.

Higher ordered bits are counted from 128, 64, 16 whereas lower ordered bits are tallied starting from 1, 2, 4...

Consequently, 30 subnets are produced by subtracting 1 from the total of 1+2+4+8+16.

which is 30-1, or 31.

We get 5 bits if we count from 1 to 16 (1, 2, 4, 8, 16).

Therefore, there are 5 borrowed bits.

How to Determine the Subnet Mask

According to the subnetting explanation above, 255.255.248.0 is unquestionably our subnet mask. But how do we get at this number?

The third octet of the subnet mask is obtained by first adding 5 higher ordered bits (128+64+32+8+4=248).

Given that the default subnet mask is 255.255.255.0 and that 5 bits were taken from the third octet (the value of the third octet is 255), we obtain the subnet mask 255.255.(128+64+32+16+8+4).0 provides us the subnet mask 255.255.248.0.

Counting the number of hosts per subnet

Remember: We chose 30 subnets for our 130.1.0.0 network right from the start of our subnetting project. The third octet's five bits were then taken. We started with only 16 bits for host addresses (the sum of bits from the third and fourth octets, each with 8 bits), because the network ID (130.1) is unchangeable. However, we only had 3 bits after taking 5 from the third octet. Thus, the third octet's 3 bits and the fourth octet's 8 bits are all that are left. We have 11 bits available for host addresses after adding the third and fourth octet bits (3+8).

The formula 2x-2, where x is the total number of possible host addresses (11), is used to determine the number of host addresses.

As a result, we arrive at 2x-2=211 -2 and 2048-2=246.

As a result, each of our subnets has 2046 hosts in it.

Identifying the Host Ranges

- As of right now, 130.1.0.0 serves as our network.

- We will use the subnet mask 255.255.248.0.

- 31 subnets.

- Each subnet, 2046 hosts.

We must go back through the process of figuring out our subnet mask in order for us to start. The third octet of our subnet mask was valued using the higher ordered bits.

Are you able to recall the lowest bit in the higher ordered set? You do, exactly like I do, for sure. It was 8. In order to retrieve the first subnet ID, we thus use the lowest of the higher ordered bits as an increment on the third octet of our network address. We then repeat this process for the next 30 subnets.

So, 130.1.8.1 to 130.1.15.254; 130.1.16.1 to 130.1.15.254; 130.1.24.1 to 130.1.15.254; etc., will be the first subnet and following subnets.

It should be noted that an address cannot contain either a zero (0) or 255 at the end.

Changing Subnet Masks

A subnet's devices MUST ALL have the same subnet mask, otherwise you may continue to experience problems with what they will and won't recognize. It doesn't matter if the mask is 255.255.255.0, 255.255.0.0, or 255.0.0.0; what matters is that each computer in that subnet has a consistent cover.

All switches and doors must have their ports organised in a way that coordinates with the subnet to which they are connected.

You can have different masks in different subnets, but you require a switch or door that is made specifically for each subnet and has two accessible ports, one on each network.

Subnet covers can be configured to isolate inside a byte even though they are typically set to isolate at each byte point. This is more difficult to implement since it depends on the double digits inside the byte.

Each subnet mask specifies the number of hosts that the system considers to be part of it; it then permits them to communicate with one another quickly but requires that all other traffic travel through a portal.

Given that you have a certain sort of door between you and the Internet and employ Network Address Translation (NAT) at that doorway, you may use any IP address range that you require within. Otherwise, you must apply for and get an appropriate open IP address class permission. It is preferable to configure a switch or tunnel with NAT and stick with the IP address provided by your ISP.

Three specific gatherings have been reserved only for internal usage. It is advised that you make use of these as Internet switches, routers, and other devices are configured NOT to advance on location inside these ranges; as a result, any traffic that unintentionally escapes is dumped at the main switch.

VLAN

The full name of VLAN is Virtual Local Area Network, sometimes known as Virtual LAN. A project team, application, or function may be used to logically partition a switched network. Users' geographic locations are not taken into account during the logical segmentation.

Physical LANs and VLANs are similar in many ways. The sole distinction is that end stations can be grouped using VLANs whether or not they are on the same physical segment.

Any type of switch module port can be accommodated by a VLAN. Only end stations inside a certain VLAN can receive relayed and swamped multicast, broadcast, and unicast data packets.

We treat each VLAN as a separate logical network. To get to their destination, packets intended for stations outside of a VLAN must be routed through a router. Notably, an IP subnet may be connected to a VLAN.

Obtainable VLANs

Traditionally, we use numbers from 1 to 4094 to designate VLANs.

You should be aware of the following:

FDDI and Token Ring VLANs each have a dedicated 1002–1005 VLAN ID.

Since they are extended-range, VLAN IDs greater than 1005 are not present in the VLAN database.

Extended-range and standard-range VLANs are supported by the switch module (1005).

The hardware of the switch module is affected by the quantity of specified features, SVIs, and routed ports.

Rules for VLAN Configuration

It's critical to comprehend the following details:

The switch module supports a total of 1005 VLANs.

Normal-range VLANs are designated by numbers between 1 and 1001.

FDDI and Token Ring VLANs are restricted to the range 1002–1006.

The switch module does not support Token Ring or FDDI.

The file holding the switch module configuration data as well as the 1–1005 VLAN IDs are typically kept in the VLAN database.

Private LAN, RSPAN VLAN, MTU, and UNI-ENI VLANs are the only ones that may use the 1006-4094 (extended-range) VLAN IDs. The VLAN database does not include these VLAN IDs.

The steps listed below will assist you in setting up or changing a VLAN:

To enter the global configuration mode, type [configure terminal].

To enter VLAN configuration mode, type [vlan vlan-id>].

To change an existing VLAN, use its VLAN ID.

To create a new VLAN, select a new ID.

Give your VLAN a name by using the command [name vlan-name>].

However, for VLANs with regular range, this is optional.

To change the MTU size, use the [mtu mtu-size>] command.

Also optional is this.

To return to privileged EXEC mode, type [end].

Use the [show vlan vlan-name | vlan-id] command.

Verify entries using the [copy running-config startup config] command.

Use the [no vlan vlan-id] command to remove a VLAN.

Keep in mind that VLAN 1 and VLANs 1002–1005 cannot be eliminated.

IPv6 vs IPv4

At the moment, IPv4 addresses are the preferred Internet IP addresses. These addresses are made up of four groups of eight bits, as was already explained. In the future, we'll probably switch to the IPv6 address format. IPv6 varies from IPv4 in two ways, both in terms of form and content:

Eight 16-bit values make up an IPv6 address, which has a total of 128 bits and is often written in four-digit hexadecimal notation. A single 16-bit number may be anything between zero and 65,535; this is a larger range than an eight-bit value.

A colon rather than a period separates the 16-bit digits in an IPv6 address.

Why switch to this? Because there aren't enough IPv4 addresses to allot one to every computer or other Internet-connected device that requires one. By providing 2 raised to the 128th power addresses, IPv6 overcomes this issue. In comparison, IPv6 only provides 2 raised to the 32nd power addresses, while masking and private-address methods have been employed to increase the amount of IPv4 addresses that are now available on the Internet.

Deal with Depletion

Depletion of IPv4 addresses is the term used to describe this. Because of the unconstrained proliferation of computer devices, the rapid expansion of the internet, and the finite number of IPv4 addresses, the IP address has always been expected. As a result of the apparent IPv4 restrictions, the introduction of IPv6 was a reaction to the IP address depletion concern.

Additionally, a variety of ideas have been developed to deal with the same problem while still using IPv4 IP addressing. The Classless Inter-Domain Routing (also known as CIDR) and Network Address Translation concepts were the most widely adopted solutions to the IP address shortage.

Protocols for Networks

Every meaningful endeavour needs clear rules and regulations that must be adhered to, as well as a step-by-step process, in order to be successful. The continual efforts to improve the networking environment through advancements in architectures and networking models have contributed to the concept's appeal.

Network protocols are a set of guidelines that guarantee efficient networking. The availability of network protocols enables access to the network services. Network protocols enable the consistency of networking standards.

We can anticipate varying applications of the networking concept given several models, notably two network types. As a result, there are apparent differences in the implementation of the TCP/IP and OSI network models, particularly in terms of the network protocols used. Understanding the network protocols that are present at each tier of the TCP/IP paradigm will be the main goal of this section.

IP Model TCP

This concept was developed far earlier than the OSI model. TCP/IP and OSI models are significantly dissimilar to one another. The TCP/IP paradigm has four levels, the lowest of which is the network connection. The other three levels are higher. The vehicle, the World Wide Web, and the layers of applications.

Each of the levels mentioned above has a different set of network protocols. Each protocol plays a certain purpose that enhances how well a layer functions overall. Connecting devices, sharing resources, and enabling network communication are the core tasks of the networking concept that are finished by the sum of the four layer functions.

Protocols At The Application Level

In the TCP/IP paradigm, this is the top layer. The process layer is another name for it. High-level protocols and representation-related challenges are covered. The layer makes it possible for users and programs to communicate.

A message is delivered to the transport layer whenever an application layer protocol needs to communicate with another application layer.

The application layer cannot be used to install all applications. Only programs that communicate with the communications network can be included in the application layer.

A web browser that supports HTTP can be installed at the application layer, but a text editor cannot. This is brought on by the browser's direct network interactions. An application layer protocol that has to be mentioned is HTTP.

Users can access information that is available on the world wide web (www) thanks to the hypertext transfer protocol.

HTTP is used to send many forms of data, including plain text, audio, and video. Because it effectively makes use of the hypertext environment, which is characterised by quick switching between different texts, it is known as the hypertext transfer protocol.

Additionally, HTTPS functions in this layer. It is an improved form of HTTP. A security protocol is HTTP over a Secure Socket Layer (HTTPS).

Wherever browsers need to complete forms, authenticate users, or conduct financial transactions, HTTPS is the best choice.

The Simple Network Management Protocol, or SNMP, is a crucial base for managing devices online. It uses the TCP/IP family of protocols.

The TCP/IP protocol known as Simple Mail Transfer Protocol, or SMTP for short, enables email services. The SMTP protocol may be used to send messages from one email account to another.

The domain name system (or simply DNS) is used to identify each host's particular IP address, which is then used to identify each host's Internet connection.

Since names are simpler to manage than addresses, many people prefer to use them instead of IP addresses. As a result, names are converted into various addresses by the DNS.

File Transfer Protocol (FTP) is a well-known internet protocol for transferring data from one computer to another over a network.

The local terminal may seem to be a terminal on the other end of the connection if two distant computers are connected via the Terminal Network (TELNET) protocol.

The following other protocols are also included in this layer:

SSH stands for Secure Shell.

X Window, NTP Network Time Protocol, and several others.

Transport Protocol Layers

This layer is comparable to the transport layer in the OSI model. It guarantees hosts' end-to-end communication. It is also in charge of making sure that data is sent without errors.

The application layer is shielded from the data complexity by the transport layer. Here is a list of the principal protocols that are available at this layer:

User Datagram Protocol (UDP) is a less expensive substitute for TCP. This protocol does not provide any of TCP's functionalities. UDP has less overhead than TCP but is less efficient as a result. As a result, it is less expensive than the TCP.

In situations when dependable transit is not a concern, UDP is the best protocol to use. It is a sensible choice. In contrast to TCP, which is connection-oriented, UDP is a connectionless protocol.

Transmission Control Protocol, a layer, guarantees dependable and error-free host-to-host communication.

Sequencing and data segmentation are handled by this layer. The transmission control protocol also has the immensely helpful acknowledgment and uses flow control algorithms to manage data flows.

Despite the fact that this layer is highly useful, the aforementioned qualities cause a significant cost. Greater implementation results from higher overhead, and vice versa.

Internet Protocol's layers

The network layer and internet layer in the OSI model carry out similar functions. At the internet layer, protocol definition takes place. The whole network's logical data transfer is handled by these protocols.

The following are the primary protocols that are accessible at the internet layer:

To function, the destination host must send data packets to the IP Protocol. The layer does this by looking for IP addresses in packet headers.

IP comes in two flavours: IPv4 and IPv6. The use of IPv4 is almost widespread. IPv6 usage is rapidly increasing since there are an endless number of IPv6 addresses as opposed to the finite number of IPv4 addresses.

ICMP, or Internet Control Message Protocol Datagrams are used to transport this protocol. It is in charge of warning the hosts of the network about any network problems.

The Address Resolution Protocol (ARP) is in charge of figuring out host addresses using well-known IP addresses.

Proxy ARP, Reverse ARP, Inverse ARP, and Gratuitous ARP are just a few of the numerous ARP variations.

Procedures For Links

The physical layer and data link layer are combined to form the link layer, commonly referred to as the network access layer in the OSI model. At this layer, hardware addressing is verified. Data can be transported physically because of the protocols employed at the network access layer.

The most used LAN technology right now is the Ethernet protocol. The OSI model's physical and data connection layers, as well as the link layer of the TCP/IP network architecture, are all places where the Ethernet protocol may be used.

The MAC and Logical Link Control (LLC) sub-layers of the TCP/IP Link Layer are necessary for the Ethernet protocol to function. The

MAC sublayer manages media access and data encapsulation, while the LLC regulates communication between lower and higher layers.

Token Ring Protocol: This protocol needs the network architecture to specify the sequence of host-to-host data transfers. A single ring links each host in the network.

A token (a 3-byte frame) is used in the token ring protocol, and it travels around the ring via a token passing mechanism. To get to their respective placements, frames move in the same manner as the token around the ring.

The acronym FDDI, or Fibre Distributed Data Interface, is used to refer to the protocol. It refers to ISO and ANSI standards that control fibre optic data transmission in local area networks (LANs). The fibre optic lines may travel up to 124 miles (200 km) in one direction.

The token ring system and the FDDI protocol both work in a similar fashion. FDDI is often used as the WANs' backbone.

There are two token rings in FDDI networks: the primary ring has a 100Mbps capacity.

the secondary ring that would be employed if the first ring failed.

It is common practice to construct WANs that allow packet-switched communications using members of the X.25 protocol family. The X.25 protocol was created in the 1970s, but it wasn't completely implemented until the 1980s.

The protocol suite is presently in great demand for use in purposeful ATM and credit card verification. A single physical line can be shared by a number of logical channels thanks to the X.25 protocol. The protocol also enables data transfer between terminals with various connection speeds.

The following 4 layers make up the X.25 protocol suite:

The physical layer describes the electrical, practical, and physical elements that link a computer to a packet-switched terminal node. Connectivity is made possible through the X.21 physical implementer.

Data link layer: The link access activities of the data link layer manage data exchange over the link. Before being transferred across the network, packets have control information attached to them. The packet layer is where the packets originate. Link Access Procedure Balanced (LAPB), which is created when the control data is added to the packets, occurs. It is possible to send frames that are bit-oriented, well-structured, and error-free utilising this type of service.

The packet layer provides ways to regulate the transmission of data packets as well as a precise definition of data packet format.

This layer provides an external virtual circuit service. There are two kinds of virtual circuits:

persistent virtual circuit The network has allocated this virtual circuit as being permanent.

Circuit for virtual calls: When necessary, a setup procedure automatically makes a virtual call. Using a call-clearing method, it ended.

The following technology elements are used to realise the X.25 concept: Data Terminal Equipment (DTE), Data Circuit Terminating Equipment (DCTE).

Implementer of X.21

Protocol for Frame Relay

Another packet-switched communication service is frame relay. It spans backbone networks, WANs, and LANs. There are two levels to it:

- Layer of data links

- Bodily layer

At the physical layer, frame relay implements all common protocols and is frequently used at the data link layer.

A virtual circuit can connect a router to a number of distant networks. Such connection is frequently made possible through permanent virtual circuits. Additionally, switched virtual circuits are an option.

Frame relay is a fast packet technique based on the X.25 standard. Data is sent by encapsulating packets into frames of various sizes. The service's high transmission rate is largely caused by a lack of mistake detection. End points carry out error-correction tasks and retransmit lost frames.

The frame relay devices are as follows:

- Equipment for Data Circuit Termination

- Equipment for Terminating Data

Address Translation for Networks

A crucial component of gateways and Internet connection devices is network address translation (NAT), which enables a computer to have an IP address that is hidden from the public Internet while being able to transmit and receive data packets over it. These addresses are concealed and allocated from a separate set of IP addresses from the ones that are visible or accessible on the Internet, known as private IP addresses. Computers behind the firewall are given private addresses that allow them to communicate with hosts on the Internet and other internal devices using TCP/IP protocols without being observed, making it more difficult to hack into the internal computer. The first line of defence against unauthorised Internet intrusion for your network PCs is to use NAT.

Because the same private, internal network IP address may be used at thousands or even millions of sites, private IP addresses also enable Internet access for more machines than there are available IP addresses.

It operates as follows: When you launch a browser to access, say, Yahoo.com, the data packet travels to your firewall or Internet gateway, which launches a session to record your MAC address and IP address.

The request is then sent to Yahoo.com, replacing your secret IP address from the data packet with its own visible IP address. The procedure is reversed when the data is returned from Yahoo for your session; the Internet gateway/firewall removes its own IP address from the packet header and replaces it with your computer's private IP address and MAC address before sending the packet down the network line to your computer.

Your internal IP address is regarded as having been "network address translated" when this occurs, while "network address substituted" could be a better description. Most home network gateways utilise NAT by default and provide every machine on the network a private IP address.

Scheduling Types

The following classes apply to routing:

Routing Static

This also goes by the name of non-adaptive routing. Routes must be manually added by the administrator to the routing database. From source to destination, packets are sent via a path that has been set by the administrator. The topology or status of the network has no bearing on routing. The administrator's responsibility is to choose the paths that data will take as they travel from source to destination.

Static Routing Advantages

The CPU consumption of the router is not impacted.

Since the administrator only has power over a certain network, there is better security.

The bandwidth between the various routers is not used.

Positive Aspects Of Static Routing

Creating a routing table for a large network is fairly taxing.

The administrator has to be very informed about networking, especially the network topology that they are working with.

Standard Routing

This method involves configuring routers such that they relay all data packets to a single hop. The network on which the hop is located is irrelevant. Simply said, packets are forwarded to the computer that is configured to receive them by default.

This method works best when a network just has to handle a single exit point. However, a router would disregard the default path and pick one that is listed in a routing table instead.

Adaptive Routing

This also goes under the name of adaptive routing. In this method, a router chooses the routing path based on the network's current circumstances.

Dynamic protocols do the bulk of the work when it comes to finding new routes. These are the RIP and OSPF protocols. In the event that a specific route does not perform as predicted, automatic changes are intended.

Guidelines for Dynamic Protocols

These characteristics of dynamic protocols are:

To swap routes, routers need to use the same protocols.

When a router notices a problem with the topology or the network condition, it broadcasts the information to all other routers that are linked.

Benefits of Dynamic Router

They are quite simple to configure.

It's the greatest choice for figuring out the optimum routes because of changes in network status and topology.

Drawbacks of Dynamic Routing

When it comes to bandwidth and CPU utilisation, it is significantly more expensive.

It is less secure than static and default routing.

Important: A router separates network traffic based on a particular protocol rather than just packet address.

A router does not physically separate a network. It does this deductively.

In order to allow specialised network traffic intended for a certain IP address to transit between designated network segments, IP routers split networks into a number of subnets. However, slower speeds are a result of this clever data forwarding.

In complicated networks, the usage of routers increases network efficiency.

Transport Protocols

Dynamic routes are those that are decided by routing protocols; the setting of routing protocols on routers facilitates the exchange of routing information.

Let's look at the many advantages that routing protocols provide.

They do away with router manual configuration. These significantly cut down on time and are a huge comfort for network admins.

Transmission of packets is unaffected by network topology changes or link loss.

Routing Protocol Types

There are two kinds of routing protocols. Here is a list of them:

Protocols for link states

protocols for vector distances

Interior Routing Protocols (IGP), which combine link state and distance vector protocols, are employed in self-governing systems to share information. The outer Routing Protocol (EGP) outer example known as Border Gateway Protocol (BGP) facilitates the exchange of routing data between internet-based autonomous systems. There is also the Cisco EIGRP protocol in addition to the ones mentioned above. Although it is simply a more sophisticated version of the distance vector protocol, some explanations refer to it as a hybrid of the two.

Protocols For A Distance

Similar to its name, the shortest route (distance) is examined to identify the optimal course.

A directly linked router using the same routing protocol (the directly linked table is referred to as a neighbour) receives the whole routing table over a distance vector protocol. EIGRP and RIP are two excellent instances of distance vector protocols.

Protocols For Link States

Link state protocols play the same function in choosing the optimum path for packet transmission as distance vector techniques do. However, they operate in a distinct manner. Link state protocols communicate network topology information rather than the entire routing table to neighbours, enabling all routers using the same protocols to eventually have topology databases that are identical.

Three different routing tables are generated by all routers using link state protocols:

Table of topology: This table includes the complete network topology.

Table for neighbours: This table includes data about neighbours who use the same protocol.

This table, known as a routing table, comprises all the recommended paths for packet transmission.

IS-IS and OSPF are two examples of link state routing protocols.

Summary

Despite having the same goal in mind, distance vector routing protocols and link state routing protocols significantly differ in how they are implemented. The obvious differences between distance vector protocols and link state routing protocols are as follows:

Link state routing systems advertise network topology information to neighbours, whereas distance vector protocols advertise the whole routing table to neighbours.

Link state routing techniques exhibit quick convergence whereas distance vector protocols exhibit delayed convergence.

Broadcasts are occasionally used by distance protocols to refresh the routing table data. On the other hand, link state routing protocols always employ multicasts to update the neighbours on the link state routing.

Compared to link state routing protocols, distance vector protocols are easier to set up.

IGRIP and RIP are two examples of distance vector routing technologies. IS-IS and OSPF are two examples of link state routing protocols.

Routing Desks

A routing table is a set of rules that are frequently given in table format to help a router or switch choose the optimum path for forwarding packets. The following characteristics define a simple routing table:

Data packets finally land at this IP address, which is the destination.

The next hop is the IP address of the device that needs to receive packets, not necessarily the end destination.

Metric: This is a cost value that is assigned to each possible route, with the lowest cost route being considered to be the ideal way.

Interface: This is the outgoing network interface that a network device should utilise to forward packets to the destination or next hop.

Routes: This is data on direct and indirect subnet information as well as default routes to use in the absence of critical data or for specific types of traffic.

Routing tables may be managed manually or automatically. Routing tables of static network devices are manually modified by a network administrator. Routing tables can be built and maintained dynamically by network devices thanks to protocols in dynamic routing.

Ports

A software endpoint that is dedicated to an application or a process is referred to as a network port. The transport layer protocols of the IP suite, such as TCP and UDP, need a port.

A port number identifies each network port. An IP address and the type of transport protocol used for communication are linked by a port number.

The port numbers are unsigned, 16-bit integers. The range of port numbers is 0 to 65535.

The Internet's Essentials

In order for everyone on your network to be able to browse the Internet, send and receive email, share digital photos, conduct research using a wealth of online resources, make purchases online, download movies and music, hold video conferences, and do much more, this section covers some of the fundamental technological concepts that underlie how the Internet functions. Also highlighted are the many ways to access the information superhighway. Let's rapidly review the history of the Internet's creation first.

Background of Google

There are a few strategic considerations to bear in mind while looking at the history of any medium, including print, broadcast, and internet. The "incredible man" idea of history, as it was formerly termed, is undoubtedly the biggest red herring for any kind of creative historicism.

This was better than more established forms of historiography, which posting lords and commanders supported, but social and financial probes have driven it out or, at the very least, eliminated it from widely verifiable records. Therefore, it would appear to be less significant to the history of the media. There is still a desire to get away from the Bells, Marconis, and Gutenbergs of any innovation. Omitting a specific "virtuoso" from mechanical, financial, and social ties is more likely to misshape a record of beginning points than explain them, even though anecdotal intricacy has its place as a nexus of recorded and material conditions. The Internet as we know it now would not have been possible without forerunners like Paul Baran and Tim Berners-Lee, nor would it have been possible without the profit-driven PC industry and the virus war.

The next issue in media history is less ostentatious but far more dangerous, especially when utilising the Internet. On the other hand, innovative determinism recognizes that major "laws" have shaped a medium's historical history, where the development of one medium creates the framework for interdisciplinary cooperation. Since the formulation of "Moore's Law," which is commonly understood to imply that PC power will double periodically or somewhere in the vicinity—Although, as we shall see, taking this particular law outside the realm of relevance creates its own problems—figuring seems especially defenceless against this kind of determinism.

Technological determinism theories, such as Manuel de Landa's War in the Age of Intelligent Machines (1991), can be helpful for escaping the humanistic tendency to put people at the centre of history, but they are unable to dispel the fallacious tendency to view innovation as an inborn advancement. Paul Levinson's Soft Edge (1997), a thorough analysis of mechanical history, uncovers some of the goals and immoral behaviours of such determinism.

According to Gary Chapman, models of mechanical history that are deterministic or value-based perform much worse than those that take into account social and material elements, particularly the willingness of institutions like markets, enterprises, and governments to invest in new media. PCs, like other machines, "are material depictions of a long process of advancement, mistake, improvement, more blunder, greater improvement, combination of highlights, the annihilation of supplanted rehearsals, scholarly achievements and impasses, etc., all encapsulated in the physical item and the way we use it" (1994:304).

Regarding radio and other forms of communication, Patrice Flichy (1995: 100) asserts that "what appears today as a progression of typically articulated advances seems to be, in general, the historical backdrop of a troublesome section starting with one space then onto the next." When arguing against the exclusion of "symptomatic advances" from social structures, Raymond Williams used TV as an example. He claimed that "symptomatic advances" are not the result of a single event or series of events, but rather depend on creations made with various closures essentially in mind for their recognition (1989:13).

Williams argues that before technologies like the telephone and electricity were valued, cultural ideas had to change.

Similar to how it was with the PC, the "Victorian Internet," which dates back to Samuel Morse's transmission of the first electric transmit message, "What hath God created?," in 1844, is now available via the Internet. Broadcast lines were set up all across Europe and North America in the ensuing decades, and the first transoceanic link was established in 1866.

With the invention of the telephone by Alexander Graham Bell in 1876, transmission linkages expanded internationally and were reinforced by phone lines, establishing the framework for the formation of a global broadcast communications system (Moschovitis et al. 1999; Standage 1998).

With the introduction of the electronic PC, this framework expanded more quickly. Charles Babbage developed and partially built his Difference Motor in the middle of the nineteenth century because he was perplexed by the challenges of thinking in what Doron Swade called "a time of evaluation." However, the standard for a broadly usable PC—ready to read, write, store, and process information—was not defined until the middle of the 20th century.

The "Turing Machine" is a mechanical computer built on the principles established by King's College, Cambridge, and Princeton University alumnus Alan Turing in his book "On Computable Numbers."

Fundamentally, Turing argued that only one out of every eight problems involving odd numbers can be solved and that there are some problems for which there is no computation that can be input into a computer. However, the bulk of problems may be input into a machine through tape, recorded, and disassembled for output when converted into a series of computerised groupings of 1s and 0s.

In the 1930s, when Turing was creating the requirements for the PC, Konrad Zuse created the Z1 and Z2, the first crude electronic computers. When constructing the Z1 in 1936, Zuse chose doubles over decimals because they could be computed more quickly. The Z1 counted parallel numerals using mechanical entryways.

These doors were replaced by the quicker electromagnetic transfers used in the Z2, but Zuse didn't finish developing a fully functional, programmable PC until the Z3 was produced in 1941. The majority of modern technology actually has a lot in common with calculating equipment. The ability to process and use a wide variety of capabilities didn't begin until the Z3 and other fully programmable electronic devices were created. Colossus and ENIAC, two computers located at the University of Pennsylvania during the Second World War, were utilised by Bletchley Park in 1943 to decipher the codes produced by the German Enigma machine.

These antique machines were massive. The IBM Mark I, Howard Aiken's Mark I, and the Manchester "Child" joined them in 1944, 1947, and 1948, respectively. The story of Grace Murray Hopper, one of the important software developers, seeing a moth in the Mark II in 1947 is where the word "bug" first appeared. Simply because they demonstrated the PC's capability for progressively increasing control, early, massive PCs like the ENIAC, which measured 650 square feet while the Mark I measured five tons, were laden with fragile vacuum cylinders and transfers.

According to John Von Neumann's hypothesis, the UNIVAC (Universal Automatic Computer) was the first commercially successful personal computer and the first of its kind to store data on a tape. The next issue was what to do with this power, and some experts have even said that the rise of these government behemoths and massive partnerships is largely to blame for the mid-20th century fixation with data concentration. Centralised computers like the System/360 and the even more powerful "supercomputers," which required enormous cabinets in unusually cold rooms manned by seasoned technocrats, dominated open reasoning in the 1950s and 1960s.

Idiom Unique To The Internet

You don't need to completely comprehend how a combustion engine operates in order to operate a car, and the same is true for using the Internet and all that it has to offer. It never hurts to quickly review the numerous phrases and ideas related to the Internet, though.

TCP/IP, or just TCP/IP for short, is a set of guidelines or protocols that specify how different pieces of technology, including computers, routers, and modems, may connect to and interact with one another. A "protocol" in this sense refers to the technical specifications for how any two communication devices would cooperate to convey digital data from one device to another.

TCP/IP operates by choosing the best transmission path. Instead of broadcasting the data all at once, the protocol divides it into small packets.

To get to their destination, where they are reassembled in the correct order, these packets might take a broad variety of pathways.

Each packet includes both the source address and the destination address to make sure it gets to the right location. These details are contained in the "header" or "envelope" of each packet.

While IP manages data packet routing, the TCP element of the protocol regulates how data is split on the sending end and reassembled on the receiving end.

Consider it this way: Data transport through TCP/IP is comparable to mailing a letter via the USPS. Both the dispatcher's (sometimes known as the source address) and the recipient's (commonly referred to as the destination address) addresses are included on every letter you mail. The main distinction between the two is that a letter is delivered by regular mail and is contained in a single box or envelope. The same letter would be sent across the Internet in dozens, hundreds, or even thousands of packets (envelopes), reaching its destination before being electronically put together.

The TCP/IP protocol suite is used to implement internet protocols including UDP, PPP, SLIP, VoIP, and FTP.

DNS

A person's name is easier to recall than her phone number, just as a website's domain name is simpler to recall than its IP address. Consider the circumstance when you routinely visit the Ford Motor Company website. Compared to its IP address, the website's domain name, Ford.com, is simpler to recall. Your computer's Web browser, however, operates in a completely different manner. The IP address of Ford.com must be known in order to access the website.

At this moment, the domain name system enters the picture. Your web browser starts a session with a DNS server, either locally or online, when you input the domain name of a website you wish to visit (for example, Ford.com), in order to get the IP address associated with that domain name. To find the IP address of the website you wish to visit, DNS servers use domain name associations for registered domain names to do a hierarchical lookup for the IP addresses. The DNS server your computer is connected to will check the number on successively higher-level DNS servers until it finds the entry (or fails) if it cannot identify the IP address associated with the domain name you submitted.

Your computer can find and contact the computer hosting the Ford.com Website once you have the IP address. In the event that you or someone else it serves has to visit that site again, the initial DNS server temporarily saves the association in memory. Only commonly used associations are stored by the DNS server since those it is unfamiliar with may be looked up on higher level DNS servers.

Root DNS servers

Using zones (controlled regions), the DNS is handled hierarchically. The root zone is the highest zone. Name-servers running in the root zone are known as DNS rooters. Direct responses to record queries for information stored in the root zone are possible from DNS root servers. Additionally, they can direct requests to the appropriate top-level domain (TLD) servers. TLD servers are hierarchically one step below root servers.

Undernet Mask

A host configuration file's use of a subnet mask enables the split of an IP class C network into discrete, routable networks. Because home networks are typically not divided into physically distinct parts with internal routers, the subnet mask for home networks connected to an ISP's larger network will most frequently be 255.255.255.0. Subnets are used to separate traffic into physically separate networks in office buildings and commercial settings in order to keep data traffic low and to improve access to local servers and peripherals. The router must be used for data traffic going to the WAN or another subnet.

World Wide Web: A Global Window

The Web is constantly changing as new networks are added or removed, much like a living thing. Every linked item now has the opportunity to communicate like never before thanks to the Internet's expansion in terms of both audience size and geographic reach. You are barely touching the surface of what can be done on the Web if your only usage of it is to download material and get email. Only one's imagination and inventiveness may restrict one's ability to utilise the Web to enlighten, educate, and share ideas, commodities, and services with a global audience. Only a small portion of what is possible on the Web is covered in this chapter.

Utilising Your Internet Connection

Your home or business network may be extended to every corner of the globe by connecting it—or a subnetwork of it—to the Internet. In the majority of areas across the nation, you can get a decently fast Internet connection with up to five static IP addresses for less than $120 per month.

These addresses can greatly improve your ability to get the most out of your Internet connection. This is due to the fact that you want at least one static IP address that is accessible through the Internet in order to make Web servers, Webcams, and other services available online. Additionally, you may utilise a static IP address to allow VPN customers to connect to the resources on your network. Much of your communication with the outside world is restricted without a static IP address. However, with a static IP address, your network can function as, to name a few, a website, client-services provider, radio station, TV station, or blog.

The Internet is a true window to the globe. Not only can you look outside, collecting vast quantities of data from the Web, but everyone in the world can see inside, allowing you to share whatever information you choose with a global audience. The Web, the ultimate unrestricted two-way, free-speech arena, may be made more useful for others while also benefiting you and your organisation by adding your own resources to it.

Common Web Purposes

The primary purposes of the internet are as follows:

Locating or Disseminating Information

The majority of people utilise the internet to find knowledge, which is why some people refer to it as the world's largest library. Search engines like Yahoo, Google, and Ask are the greatest places to start when looking for information online.

One or more links to Web pages related to the word or phrase you entered are returned when you enter a word or phrase in the search bar on any of these websites. What details about you, your family, or your business should be put to a Web server? This is a question you should ask yourself or the management of your firm.

It takes more than just purchasing a domain name like thisismywebsite.com to make your information or voice heard online. You include relevant search terms in the headers of your documents to make sure they can be seen when someone does a connected search, and you could pay to register your website with many search engines. It's a science in and of itself to learn important search terms and modify your document headers and labels accordingly. And even if you are an expert at it, your company's website may rank first one day and fall to 100 or

1,000 the next. Similar to the Wild West, there aren't many regulations online, and everything goes if you want to stand out.

Communication

These are the ways that this happens:

E-mail

E-mail, in which messages are electronically transferred from sender to host on the Internet, maybe forwarded to other sites, and eventually retrieved at the recipient's convenience, is the most common form of Internet communication.

Your Internet service provider (ISP) is one place to get an email account; most plans come with the usage of at least one email address. As an alternative, you might manage your own personal or professional email server using a domain name you control. Through specialised software known as an email client, you may access messages sent through these accounts.

Another choice is to utilise any of the many free web-based email services available today, like the ones listed below:

Yahoo! Mail is available at mail.yahoo.com.

Gmail is available at www.gmail.com.

SMS (Short Message Service)

Instant messaging (IM) is a different method of online communication. Quick messaging (IM) allows for quick communication; there is no mediator needed to store or send the message. When both end users are online and press the Send button (or a similar button), the text they are typing is instantaneously communicated from one to the other in a back-and-forth method.

Using a desktop IM client or, in certain situations, a web browser, you can IM. A few common instant messaging programs are as follows:

Window Live Messenger, Yahoo! Messenger

Visual Conference

Those that utilise video conferencing have the unique opportunity to have meetings virtually, which helps them save money on transportation. At least one participant must have a static IP address that is visible to the Internet in order to conduct a video conference over the Internet. In order to maintain high-quality connections, especially if you're using the video component, each contributor should have a service with an upload speed of at least 400Kbps. You must have access to some kind of Webcam in order to video conference.

Weblogs, often known as blogs, are websites where users may exchange information with others who share their interests or a similar perspective. Consider a blog as an online journal that is accessible to readers anywhere.

The Media and Entertainment

There are a ton of entertainment alternatives available on the Internet, including the following:

engaging video games

Internet radio station for music and news

TV on the internet

Taking Part in Business

One of the most popular applications of the Internet is for business. Business-related activities can also include, but are not limited to:

Retail marketing and sales

Financial auctions

Advertising

Obtaining Software

Users have the option to download what would otherwise be boxed commercial off-the-shelf (COTS) software from a number of large software providers, including Microsoft, Corel, and Sun. All you need to pay the price is a strong Internet connection, a PayPal account, a credit card, or even a chequebook. Additionally, there is a substantial selection of open-source software, freeware, shareware, and trial software that may be downloaded online.

Surveillance

As long as you have the correct IP addresses for the web servers or cameras, setting up security cameras so that they can be watched online is practically plug-and-play. Using this technology, you may check on your vacation home while you're at home or monitor your office while you're abroad.

Business owners can install cameras at their workplace to watch over activities there or to keep an eye on things while they're gone.

Internet service plan evaluation

A minimum of one Internet-capable computer on your network and the purchase of an Internet service package from an Internet service provider (ISP) are prerequisites for setting up home Internet access. The types of plans that are available depend partially on your location (urban regions often have more possibilities than suburban and rural ones), the communication mediums you wish to utilise, and the choices made by your ISP.

Among important plan components are the following:

Internet flow

Support for customer service

addresses for email

Price ISP-supplied equipment

given IP address type: static or dynamic

Free Wi-Fi is available.

utilised transmission medium

hosting a website

How to Connect to the Internet

You must select one of the service-plan choices offered in your region in order to connect your computer to the Internet. Once you have chosen an ISP and have assessed the connection packages and media options available in your region, have a look at some of the tips listed below for advice on how to set up Internet access.

Dial-Up Internet

In terms of speed, dial-up is mostly no longer used, but in certain rural regions, it remains the only low-cost Internet connection option. There are three typical circumstances when dialling up to your computer via an analog phone connection (POTS):

connecting a laptop or PC with a built-in modem

using a USB port to link an external dial-up modem

use a 9-pin serial port-compatible modem.

Utilising Cables

Cable is a common option for Internet access in many places. In fact, a cable connection for television service may already be present in your house or small business, making the addition of a cable modem to the mix rather easy. Dial-up Internet service cannot compare to the high speed provided by cable. Many cable-based bundles now provide Internet phone connectivity in addition to more television channels for viewing.

Wi-Fi use

It's quite easy to connect wirelessly to the Internet, but your network has to have a gateway or router built for wireless connections. Additionally, any computer connected to your network has to have Wi-Fi capability, or if it's a laptop or notebook, a slot for a wireless Wi-Fi card.

Do not worry if your PC or workstations are not Wi-Fi setup. Numerous companies provide products that offer wireless connections; in essence, these products are portable wireless NICs that can be connected into either an Ethernet port or a USB port.

DSL use

If you reside in a region where DSL service is offered, connecting to the internet using DSL over regular phone lines provides the advantage of faster access speeds than dial-up. Furthermore, whereas a dial-up connection relies on the audio/analog band on a phone line, data from a DSL Internet connection travels over the wire pair at a frequency that is higher, allowing users to continue using their phone lines while using the Internet (and, by extension, maintaining your Internet connection 24/7).

Virtualization And Cloud Computing Architecture

Cloud Computing Meaning, Delivering IT resources over the internet in response to demand is known as cloud computing. Typically, a pay-as-you-go pricing model is used in conjunction with it. Cloud computing aims to satisfy clients' demands for low-cost IT infrastructure.

The Cloud Computing Process

A server is often necessary for small and large IT firms that continue to carry out their various activities using traditional techniques. It takes specialised workers, several servers, modems, switches, and a ton of other networking hardware to set up a server room. There are several more non-IT requirements that are crucial for an office to function well.

Traditional techniques need a lot of work, pricey equipment, and additional logistical requirements. These items are really pricey. A company or individual must be willing to spend a lot in order to put up a fully effective server. Due to the idea of cloud computing, this is no longer the case. By removing the need to spend a lot of money on labour costs to administer and maintain IT resources, cloud computing enables people to save money on infrastructure expenditures.

Knowledge Of Cloud Computing

A distributed computing environment is utilised by cloud computing. This enables efficient resource exchange.

The usage of several servers in cloud computing reduces the possibility of infrastructure failure. It becomes a more dependable infrastructure for IT operations as a consequence.

Thanks to cloud computing, which enables the provision of enormous amounts of on-demand IT resources, engineers and a number of other specialists are not required.

Since cloud computing makes use of the same infrastructure, numerous users may share resources and work more efficiently.

With cloud computing, users may access resources and systems from anywhere, eliminating the need to contend with issues related to distance or physical location.

Maintenance is made simpler by the absence of the need for program installation on each user's PC.

Because a firm does not have to spend on creating its own infrastructure, which is sometimes rather expensive for most enterprises, operational expenses are decreased. Furthermore, it enables a corporation to only spend money on resources or services that are really utilised.

Pay-per-use business models are made possible for many businesses by cloud computing. When a user just needs to access a resource once, it is a helpful tactic to employ.

Use of Cloud Computing

It is possible to have only one application where all users may log in and get the services they need rather than installing a whole pricey software suite on every employee's PC. Users of the program get access to a web-based service that has all the programs they need to carry out their job. Every task will be carried out by remote servers under the management and supervision of a third party. Cloud computing is now in use.

In cloud computing, most labour-intensive operations are not finished by local workstations. On distant servers, even the most complex software is executed and vast amounts of data are stored. These reduce the amount of hardware and software the user needs. An interface program for cloud computing can be run on even a cheap system. Due to the fact that the great majority of software can be accessible via the cloud, cloud computing also does away with the requirement to purchase it.

Virtualization

Making a virtual replica of anything real is referred to as virtualization. This can happen in computing when an operating system, network resources, server, storage device, or even a desktop is virtualized.

In terms of technology, virtualization is a method that enables a number of individuals or groups to share a single instance of a physical resource or program.

providing a specific resource or application a reference and providing the physical storage of a specified resource or application a logical name are both steps in the process.

Virtualization Types

The several virtualization subcategories are shown below.

Server virtualization is the process of installing virtual machine management (VMM), or software for virtual machines, directly on the server.

What justifies virtualizing servers?

Server virtualization is crucial for load balancing and the ability to split a physical server into as many servers as required.

Storage virtualization is the act of combining many physical storage devices into a single entity that functions as a storage unit via a network. Storage virtualization is also implemented using software programs.

Why virtualize storage, one may ask?

This is essential for backup and recovery purposes.

operating system virtualization: In this scenario, the virtual machine management (VMM) software is installed right away by the host computer's operating system. Unlike hardware virtualization, which necessitates hardware installation, VMM does not.

Why virtualizing operating systems is a good idea.

When testing software on a separate operating system platform is necessary, operating system virtualization is useful.

Software for virtual machines is put directly on the hardware system in hardware virtualization. The hypervisor is in charge of controlling and keeping track of the hardware, memory, and CPU, among other physical resources. We may install several operating systems and run a number of additional apps on the virtualized version of the real machine.

Why virtualize hardware, one may ask?

Because controlling virtual computers is easier than managing actual servers, hardware virtualization is crucial for server systems.

Vulnerability In Cloud Computing

In cloud computing, virtualization is a tremendously powerful idea. Users frequently share the resources available in cloud computing. Two examples of shared resources that may be kept in the cloud are apps and data. Users are given a platform that allows sharing of these resources through virtualization.

Giving users cloud access to software in its conventional forms is virtualization's primary purpose. Customers want fresh versions of their favourite apps from a software developer. This is conceivable, however if everyone had to download the updated version from a central server, it would be quite stressful. Cloud customers can easily acquire the most recent software updates, however virtualized servers and software can be maintained by third parties for a charge to remedy that issue.

In conclusion, virtualization is just sharing all hardware resources across many operating systems running on a single computer.

This strategy offers a number of benefits since it makes it simple and economical to combine network resources and distribute them across many users.

a server computer's parts

The primary parts of a server computer are as follows:

storage equipment

on the motherboard, the processor Internet connection

VGA devices

Source of Memory Power

The most common and well-liked virtualization programs are as follows:

Oracle QEMU is used for Fusion for VMWare Parallels Desktop and VMWare Workstation virtualization.

Mac version of Redhat Virtualization Veertu Apple-Boot Microsoft Hyper-V Camp

Three Categories of Fundamental Cloud Services

Online users may get cloud services on demand thanks to cloud computing. Among the most used cloud services are the following:

Amazon Web Services

Google Windows Azure Cloud

Public And Private Cloud Comparison

The fundamental difference in management between a public cloud hosting solution and a private cloud hosting.

Utilising Public Cloud Services

In a public cloud hosting solution, user data is managed and stored by a cloud provider. The data centres that cloud service companies maintain house their clients' sensitive information. Many people like this option since public cloud hosting is more economical in terms of management. Some people think that there is a larger chance that the safety and security of data stored in a public cloud may be compromised. Though the requirement imposed on the cloud provider from a business and legal standpoint could just be enough of a motivator to enhance the security and safety of their clients' data.

Private Cloud Services

Private cloud hosting options offer the upkeep and management of a cloud service under the direction and control of a particular business. A private cloud hosting system is also known as a company cloud or internal cloud. A business or group manages its own cloud service from behind a firewall. Even while private cloud hosting choices may offer a higher level of data confidentiality and safety, the infrastructure requirements may prove to be prohibitively expensive. Highly qualified personnel must be engaged to manage the cloud. As a result, a company or organisation will incur increased running costs.

Network Troubleshooting

All problems relating to the following must be addressed for effective network management:

Hardware management and customer service

administration of software data

Hardware Administration and Upkeep

The following procedures and considerations can be followed while doing hardware maintenance:

Cleaning

Clean all network hardware twice a month. By doing this, you'll be able to keep your equipment cold and do other maintenance duties more easily. Dust the machinery, the shelves, and the surrounding surroundings when cleaning. The computer vent and fan apertures, as well as the keyboards, should be vacuumed using a tiny vacuum. You should also use the vacuum to delicately remove dust from removable media drives. You can also sometimes vacuum empty equipment jacks and unused wall jacks in dusty areas.

Follow the handbook instructions for cleaning print heads on inkjet printers and vacuuming paper dust from laser printers when using printers and plotters. With the use of glasses cleaning solutions and wipes, monitors may be cleaned.

Carrying out inspections

It's crucial to keep a careful check on the state of all gear. This calls for a minimum monthly hardware inspection schedule. The following should be checked during this inspection:

Make that the vents for the cooling system are not clogged or too dusty.

To confirm that cooling fans are running, listen to the vents and feel them.

sniff around. Power supply and other components may release an unpleasant stench due to overheating when they are on the verge of failing. Trouble is either about to or has already occurred when there is a burning scent.

Verify that all network, peripheral, and power cables are securely seated in their sockets.

Check for fraying or other damage on any network cables, peripheral cables, and power cables.

Even though those systems are not required at the time of the inspections, make sure they are operational by checking the server area's heating, ventilation, and cooling systems for correct operation.

Changing the Firmware

Any software that is stored on a chip is referred to as "firmware". The BIOS of a computer is an example of firmware. Manufacturers occasionally offer firmware updates to address bugs or make the equipment compatible with freshly released hardware or operating-system upgrades. To find out if any firmware updates are available for your equipment, you should at least quarterly visit the manufacturer's website or help desk.

If so, be sure to load fresh firmware and firmware upgrades according to the maker's instructions exactly. Some firmware loading will work with the computer's operating system, while many need low-level booting from a DOS or maintenance CD.

Hardware Upgrades

Hardware advancements are driven by two factors:

A hardware update or the inclusion of additional features tied to the capabilities or capacity of the hardware may be required to address performance concerns brought on by changes in applications or the addition of new apps. For instance, common modifications to accommodate those changes include boosting RAM and installing an extra hard drive for greater storage capacity.

You can choose to improve your hardware solely at your discretion, for example by installing a larger display, a better sound card, a TV card, or another comparable device.

Mechanics of Hardware

You must evaluate your readiness and capacity to handle hardware repairs as the person in charge of the network before a hardware component breaks down. To that aim, you must examine all of your hardware stock and decide the following:

Is the machinery still covered by the warranty? If so, in the event that the equipment breaks down, make use of that warranty.

Would replacing a broken piece of hardware immediately be more economical? Repairing cheap equipment, such as a printer that can be replaced for $50, may not be justifiable given the high cost of technical labour. If you've had a PC for more than ten months and paid less than $600 for it, it could even be advisable to replace it rather than get it fixed. Please understand that I do not support reducing the lifespan of equipment or needlessly increasing scrap piles.

If your budget allows, you might wish to set up service and support contracts for expensive equipment to transfer the repair risk to a third party.

Troubleshooting A Network

The term "network trouble-shooting" refers to all the steps and methods put together to locate, recognize, and fix network problems. The methodical procedure's main goal is to get a computer network operating normally again.

In order to guarantee a smooth functioning of the network, network administrators are tasked with the duty of locating and fixing network issues. Additionally, they go above and above to guarantee that the network is performing at its peak.

Among the numerous computer network troubleshooting techniques are the following:

switching and router setup, as well as any other network component configuration.

locating any network problems and devising a solution.

Wi-Fi equipment as well as network cable installation and repair.

cleaning up the network of malware.

updating the firmware on your devices.

Software can be installed and removed as necessary.

Both manual and automatic methods can be used for network troubleshooting, particularly when dealing with network software applications. In order to identify network problems that could be difficult to see with the naked eye, network diagnostic software is a useful tool.

Both hardware and software troubleshooting are included in network troubleshooting.

Hardware Diagnostics

This method of troubleshooting deals with problems involving hardware parts. It might contain:

Removal of defective or damaged RAM, NIC, or hard drive

Dusting computer and other network equipment is necessary because accumulated dust can occasionally cause equipment failure.

wire tightening between various network components

installation or updating of crucial hardware drivers

The first step in hardware troubleshooting is to identify a specific hardware problem, identify its root cause, and then take the appropriate corrective action.

Network Management Synopsis

Large networks frequently include one or more employees who are solely responsible for handling network administration duties. For smaller networks, the management must play many different jobs and wear many different hats. To succeed, he or she must eventually advance to the rank of journeyman, or at the very least, experienced apprentice.

One of the following categories best describes primary or routine network administration tasks:

Managing and assisting end users

Including workstations and other equipment

upkeep of the system's documentation

The Upkeep Of System-Wide Documentation

It might seem like you could forgo maintaining system-wide documentation, but you shouldn't. Without thorough documentation, you risk wasting a lot of man hours when something goes wrong, when you're trying to add hardware to a server, or when you're attempting to add software to network hosts or workstations. Unfortunately, reading the documentation before making system modifications is not always prioritised by technicians and network administrators. The fact that good documentation techniques require time does not make them a curse; rather, they are a benefit to the network manager who has limited spare time.

The manuals for all the hardware as well as any operation and maintenance guides should be included in the network documentation.

Managing and Assisting End-Users

End-user administration and assistance will probably fall within your purview as the network administrator. The following is an example of a task you may need to complete:

new users being screened for security

End-user account creation, deletion, and modification

establishing and managing individual, group, and role-based access restrictions

Giving technological assistance

Including workstations and other equipment

Workstations and Peripheral Devices Addition

It's possible that there may be instances when adding additional workstations and peripheral devices to the network requires performing certain software-based administrative tasks. Examples include adding a new printer to a print server's queue or hardcoding an IP address into a new computer or printer. In addition, it may be necessary to give users access to passwords for new network workstations as well as permissions to utilise new devices like printers. Consult your own records of the processes required for past adjustments and the paperwork included with the new equipment for further details.

Software Troubleshooting Software refers to a collection of procedures for identifying, diagnosing, and providing fixes for software-related problems in networks. Problems with network operating systems, diagnostic tools, and software programs installed on specific network machines are all covered.

Troubleshooting Cable

A physical link between network components is provided via cabling. Physical interference can interfere with cables. As a result, there might be connection interruption as a result of outside pressure. They might also sustain harm. Numerous problems might develop when this type of interference happens since interference with wires directly affects the transfer of data. Thus, since data transfer is impeded, cable problems invariably result in a communication breakdown.

In order to ensure that network operations are not disrupted, at least not for an extended period of time, network administrators must be able to recognize cable problems and be prepared to give swift remedies.

Wireshark Quick Reference

The software used to analyse network traffic in real time is free and open-source. Both administrators and professionals in network security should use it. It aids in the investigation of network problems such as lost packets, latency problems, and hostile activity on networks. In-depth networking expertise is required to utilise Wireshark efficiently. Users who use Wireshark should be familiar with the TCP/IP protocol, be able to read and interpret packet headers, and be knowledgeable with the routing, DHCP, and port forwarding processes, among other things.

Just How Does Wireshark Operate?

Wireshark swiftly transforms network traffic into a human readable format after it has been captured. This makes it easier for network managers to monitor the kind and volume of network traffic.

Capture filters only gather the types of traffic that have been expressly designated by the network administrator in order to prevent dealing with too much needless traffic.

With the help of Wireshark's capabilities, it is possible to create baseline statistics that separate what is "abnormal" from what is "normal."

Conclusion

Anyone hoping for a meaningful experience in the sometimes difficult field of computer networking should start by thoroughly comprehending the fundamental networking ideas. Every ambitious student sets off on their road with a desire to learn more after receiving a succinct, accurate, and compassionate introduction to networking. The first chapter stands out as an overview of networking fundamentals that equips the reader to comprehend increasingly complicated networking topics with ease and speed. The OSI reference model, peer-to-peer network designs, and a fundamental understanding of the many network types and network components all contribute to a speedy but thorough education of the reader of what to anticipate in terms of networking.

The concept of networking does not necessarily appeal to networking specialists or would-be networking experts. Users of computer networks have the unusual chance to arm themselves with information about the intricacies of what they periodically engage with — the computer network — even if they merely require the technical know-how to navigate different types of computer networks for their own aims.

As is commonly recognized among networking fans, a toddler must first crawl before standing up, take a little step before walking out into the street. Unquestionably, this book provides a thorough introduction to the fundamentals of computer networking by laying out the necessary networking ideas before teaching a beginner-friendly instruction on network design and operation.

The reader is given a clear impression of the fascinating future of networking studies through a few more or less complex topics relating to network management and security, the Internet, and virtualization in cloud computing.

Don't miss out!

Visit the website below and you can sign up to receive emails whenever Book Wave Publications publishes a new book. There's no charge and no obligation.

https://books2read.com/r/B-A-LAFAB-IXNOC

Connecting independent readers to independent writers.

Also by Book Wave Publications

How To Make Money In Stocks Value Investing Strategies
Master The Steps To Move Away From The Past And Following Inspiration
Heartful Journeys: Exploring The Power Of Mindful Living
Essential Computer Networking Concepts You Should Know
Harnessing Your Inner Strength Overcoming Limiting Beliefs
Mastering Networking Basics From Novice To Pro